KEEPING THE MISSION
IN THE MISSIONARY

THE PAULINE MODEL
OF MISSIONS
IN PHILIPPIANS

BY JEFF AMSBAUGH

Keeping the Mission in the Missionary
By Jeff Amsbaugh

©2002 Jeffrey Alan Amsbaugh
Grace Baptist Church
2915 Fourteenth Avenue
Columbus, Georgia 31904

DEDICATION

To Don Sisk,
Pat Creed,
and Fred Moritz,
three men who
have enflamed my
passion for missions
— Philippians 4:18

ACKNOWLEDGMENTS

I wish to thank Mrs. Becky Crouch, who served as my secretary during the composition of this manuscript and who worked tirelessly and efficiently to put it into the computer.

I also wish to thank Mrs. Holly Wismer who served as the proofreader for the dissertation and Mrs. Bessie Barrick who served as proofreader for its adaptation into book form.

Special thanks is also due to Cyde McQuien for his superb cover design.

Table of Contents

Chapter 1
There's a Missionary Holding on Line One

Pastors frequently receive telephone calls from missionaries who desire to raise support to get to the mission field. Obviously, these pastors cannot lead their church to support every missionary who requests assistance. Only a certain amount of money is available in each local church, and though pastors would like to help more missionaries get to the field, it is not always financially possible.

Even if these local churches have the money to support those who request funds, it would not always be in the best interest of the missionary or the church to do so. Some missionaries are not ethical in their ministry practices. Some missionaries are not sound theologically, and other missionaries, simply because of their personalities, "create a stir" every time they come home to report on their efforts. These issues and others necessitate that a church be selective in organizing its missionary program.

This selectivity should be based on major Biblical principles rather than on minor differences of personal standards. Some missionaries have been rejected for support because they owned televisions, their wives wore slacks, or the school from which they graduated held to the critical text of Scripture. On the other hand, some missionaries who compiled with these standards were found to have a spirit of anger or hostility that was detrimental on the mission field. How should a church determine who it will or will not support?

A Look at Acts

Many pastors have turned to the book of Acts for guidance, and indeed the Pauline model in Acts has much to commend itself. From this model, the importance of evangelism has been stressed. Missionaries are not primarily philanthropists and humanitarians; they are evangelists. The goal of the missionary is not to produce a healthy body that will be thrown into hell (Matthew 5:29). While the Gospel does have social ramifications, missionaries must not preach a social gospel.

The Pauline model in Acts has also stressed the importance of discipleship and church planting. Spiritual "infanticide" has been rampant in some circles, where "spiritual babies" are "birthed" only to be left alone. The need to develop these converts and congregate them into local churches is imperative. A return to the Pauline model in Acts has brought the importance of the local church back into the focus of missionary activity. For this, the Lord should be praised.

The Pauline model in Acts has also helped to lessen much bigotry in missions by encouraging trust in national pastors. Many missionaries now view their task as one of training nationals to take their place. They believe that a good missionary tries to "work himself out of a job." As a result, numerous seminaries and Bible colleges have been started around the globe for the express purpose of training national pastors. Once these national pastors are in place, the churches they lead are viewed as autonomous and free of the need for American interference. By going back to the book of Acts, a trust in national leadership has been reborn.

The Pauline Model in Acts Fails to Address Missionary Character

Yet for all the strengths of the Pauline model in Acts, several weaknesses still exist. The first weakness is that this model does nothing to address the character of the missionary. Many missionaries have proven themselves to be philosophically correct, yet personally deficient. It is possible that the candidate may have a Scriptural philosophy of ministry and not be spiritual. The Pauline model in Acts does nothing to address the character of the missionary himself, and difficulties arise when a missionary tries to implement spiritual principles when he himself is carnal.

The Pauline Model in Acts Is Based on Narrative

A second major weakness of this model is that it comes from historical narrative, rather than a didactic epistle. As John MacArthur states, "Evangelical theologians have drawn the heart of their doctrine from Bible passages penned expressly to teach the church. They have understood Acts as an inspired historical record of the apostolic period, not necessarily viewing every event or phenomenon there as normative for the entire church age."[1] If charismatics are criticized for developing their theology of the Spirit from the book of Acts, how can one in good conscience develop his theology of missions from the same narrative sections? How can one determine which parts of Paul's missionary work were only for the apostolic era and which parts are normative for the entire church age? These questions cannot be answered easily, and therefore, it is imperative to consult the epistles.

---

[1]John MacArthur, Jr., Charismatic Chaos (Grand Rapids: Zondervan Publishing House, 1992), 171.

A Look at Philippians

Is there a didactic epistle that is missiological in its thrust? Philippians appears to focus on missions. The planting of the church at Philippi, described in Acts 16:12-40, marked the entrance of the Gospel into Europe. Luke describes the city as a Roman "colony" and "the chief city of that part of Macedonia."[2] The Acts narrative testifies to the presence of a Jewish community before Paul and his missionary friends arrived (Acts 16:13). The apostle addressed his message to some Jewish women who met for prayer, and the Lord opened the heart of a woman named Lydia.

Two other conversion stories from Philippi are reported in the book of Acts, and these make it clear that Paul did not restrict the Gospel to Jews in this city. Ralph Martin observes that "two notable conversions from the world of paganism are graphically recorded, the slave-girl (16:16-18) and the Roman jailer (vv. 19-34)."[3] In addition, the names of the church members in the letter (2:25; 4:2-3) reveal that many of the converts were pagan Gentiles, in spite of the fact that the church met in Lydia's house (Acts 16:40). Thus the main influx into the church was from the Gentile world. In the midst of this "crooked and perverse nation" (2:15), Paul planted a church.

This ministry was one of the most significant of Paul's missionary accomplishments. He remembers vividly "the first day" (1:5) that the Philippians joined him in the

---

[2]All Scripture quotations, unless otherwise noted, are from the Authorized King James Version.

[3]Ralph P. Martin, <u>The Epistle of Paul to the Philippians</u> (Grand Rapids: Eerdmans Publishing Company, 1987). 19.

fellowship of the Gospel. Because those days were the beginning of Paul's Gospel-preaching attempts (4:15), they made a lasting impression on him. Paul looked upon the Philippian believers with great satisfaction (4:1) and bragged about them to other churches (2 Corinthians 8:1).[4]

Specifically, this boasting centered on the giving nature of the church at Philippi. Throughout the Philippian letter (1:3, 5; 4:10, 14ff.), Paul acknowledges his gratitude for the repeated generosity of this church. In spite of their poverty-stricken circumstances, they gave material help to the apostle from the time he left the city. At Thessalonica, and again at Corinth, gifts from the Philippian believers reached him. In this way the Philippian epistle is a missionary prayer letter, thanking a supporting church for its continued financial faithfulness.

A Look at Paul

D. Edmond Hiebert has called Paul's letter to the Philippians "an open window into the Apostle's very heart."[5] The epistle is intensely personal, with all the marks "of a free and spontaneous letter to beloved friends." In it, Paul opens his heart and affections to the Philippians. He mentions himself more often than in any of his other epistles. The first person singular pronoun, either alone or in the Greek verb, occurs no less than 120 times in Philippians. It has the free, personal flow of a letter to intimate friends.[6]

---

[4]Martin, 19.

[5]D. Edmond Hiebert, <u>An Introduction to the Pauline Epistles</u> (Chicago: Moody Press, 1954), 283.

[6]Hiebert, 296.

The book of Philippians, therefore, gives more insight into Paul as a man than any other New Testament book. The personal testimony of the missionary comes shining through the entire epistle. The letter was written to provide the Philippian church with information concerning his person. Because Paul was imprisoned, the Philippians were anxious to get the latest information about his case. The apostle does not disappoint them. One learns more about Paul from Paul in this book than in any other. For this reason, the book of Philippians provides an excellent source for learning about the psychological and spiritual makeup of a successful missionary and thus provides a useful tool for developing an instrument for evaluating those who are called to the field as missionaries.

This correspondence from Paul is "missionary" in many aspects. It was written to a church that was planted by a missionary to thank them for their financial participation in missions. Because these things are true, one can expect to find significant missiological principles within its contents. Using this inspired missionary prayer letter as a guide, how can a missionary candidate be evaluated during pre-field ministry?

It is anticipated that the Philippian model, as opposed to the Acts model, will produce more than just a philosophy of ministry. It is also hoped that the Philippian model will reveal principles about the missionary himself, leading to the development of an instrument to help the church evaluate the personal life of the missionary candidate while at the same time helping the missionary appointee to assess his life before going to the mission field. These goals demand certain avenues of exploration.

Interpersonal Relationships

First, what can be discovered about the missionary's interpersonal relationships? Numerous authors have revealed that many new arrivals on the mission field become disillusioned, not by the pagan culture of the country where they have surrendered to serve, but by the missionaries from America who are already there. Missionaries, like all others, struggle with interpersonal relationships. Most importantly, how does the missionary view his relationship with Jesus Christ? How does he view his relationship with saints generally? What is his attitude toward his supporting local churches? How does he handle the lost whom he has been called to evangelize?

The opening section of the book (Philippians 1:1-2) gives some insight into Paul's interpersonal relationships. It explains Paul's relationship to Jesus Christ, his relationship to his co-worker Timothy, his relationship to saints generally, and his relationship to his supporting church at Philippi particularly. What can the missionary candidate learn from Paul in his attitude toward others?

Surrender and Commitment

Many pastors have led their congregations to adopt particular missionary families for support, only to discover that these families would not finish deputation. Others, while finishing deputation, only last for one term on the mission field. Is there any way a church can ascertain the commitment level of a missionary appointee prior to his departure? Can the church find out if the candidate views his choice to go to the mission field as merely a good and spiritual option, or does he sense that God has called him and that "there is no turning back?" Does the Philippian model provide any means of ascertaining a missionary's surrender and commitment level?

After his salutation, Paul expresses his thanksgiving and confidence (Philippians 1:3-7). Paul the missionary was bursting with confidence. Here was no half-hearted surrender. Can Baptist missionary candidates say that they are "confident of this very thing" (Philippians 1:6)?

Prayer Life

There can be little doubt that prayer is an important element in the life of the Christian, especially the missionary. The ability to handle culture shock, to get along with fellow missionaries, to be effective in evangelism, and to avoid discouragement can all be traced directly or indirectly to the prayer life of the missionary. Does the Philippian model provide any means by which a candidate's prayer life can be evaluated?

The book of Philippians reveals something about the nature of the Apostle Paul's prayer life (Philippians 1:8-11). As Martin states, "We may be sure that the apostle availed himself of his own secret of inward peace and tranquility by the resources of prayer and petition."[7] Does the missionary candidate's faith in and attitude toward prayer mirror what we find in the Apostle Paul?

Commitment Level

During annual church missionary conferences, the glorious prospect of missionary activity is presented.

---

[7]Ralph P. Martin, The Epistle of Paul to the Philippians (Grand Rapids: Eerdmans Publishing Company, 1987), 46.

Evangelized, discipled, and congregated nationals are shown in slide presentations. Edited from these presentations, however, are the numerous heartaches, failures, and disillusionments that the missionary encountered along the way. The new missionary quickly discovers that the mission field is not as grand and glorious as the missionary conference led him to believe. He may become discouraged. Is there any way that the local church can evaluate the contentment level of a missionary before he departs? How will he be able to face and handle defeat on the field?

Because of his missionary activity, the Apostle Paul found himself in jail. His initial entrance into Philippi resulted in imprisonment (Acts 16:23), and now years later, writing back to the Philippian church, Paul is in jail again (Philippians 1:13). How did the apostle remain contented when so many terrible things happened to him? His answer in Philippians 1:12-26 is the basis for a useful piece of the instrument used to evaluate any missionary candidate.

Pulpit Ministry

Many American Christians think that if a preacher is an inadequate pulpiteer, he surrenders to go to the mission field. Unfortunately, many missionary candidates have done nothing to dispel this misconception. If a missionary fails to hold the attention of an audience who speaks his native tongue and shares his culture, how will he hold the attention of an audience that is linguistically and culturally diverse? What topics should characterized the missionary's sermon? Should he be known for a fantastic sermon condemning television when he is going to a culture that has no electricity? How can the local church evaluate the pulpit ministry of the missionary appointee?

Paul the missionary was also a preacher. How did Paul use the pulpit? What did he consider important for the local church to know? What was the central message that he preached? Paul's exhortations to the believing community in Philippi (Philippians 1:27-2:18) give us some ideas as to Paul's philosophy of preaching, and these ideas will prove helpful in evaluating the preaching of missionary candidates.

Vision for the Future

American pastors frequently take existing churches with existing programs and bring those churches and programs to new heights. The missionary, on the other hand, frequently must start "from scratch." Church planting is the creation of something out of nothing. This requires vision. Does the missionary candidate have the ability to see what is not presently there? Does he have the faith to visualize that which does not presently exist? How does the local church evaluate the vision that this candidate has for the future?

The Apostle Paul was often planning for the future, and the book of Philippians is no exception. Once again Paul communicates his vision for the months ahead (Philippians 2:19-30). How did Paul view the future? What can present-day missionary candidates learn form this visionary?

Educational Background

Some mission boards require at least a degree from a recognized Bible college. Some strongly suggest a master's degree. Others believe that "the world is perishing by degrees," and all that a missionary needs is the call of God in his heart and a Bible in his hand. Is educational background important? Does the answer vary depending upon the particular field of service? How does the local church evaluate whether the missionary's educational background is sufficient for the field to which he has been called?

In the book of Philippians, Paul tells the reader something about his background that prepared him for the mission field (Philippians 3:1-14). Using Paul as the standard, one can evaluate current missionary candidates. Are they unprepared for the field? Would it be wise for some local churches to recommend further training for prospective missionaries? Is it possible that some missionaries, though called, are not ready yet to fulfill that calling? What does Paul's educational background say about current theological educational systems?

Philosophy of Separation

Numerous missionaries have reported that when they arrived on the field, the cultists had arrived first. Jehovah Witnesses and Mormons preceded them. In addition, many mission fields, especially those in Latin and South America, are saturated with Catholicism. Charismatics are found in numerous locations around the world. What will the missionary's attitude be toward these divergent groups of Christendom? Will his policy be one of complete separation? What will he do with his evangelical brothers who are not apostates but choose to fellowship with apostates? How important is separation on the mission field?

Though the Apostle Paul worked for unity and constantly stressed it, he recognized the necessity of separation (Philippians 3:15-21). What do the missionary candidates who come to our local churches believe about separation? Is this an important issue for the missionary? With whom do we fellowship, and from whom do we separate? The Philippian model provides some helpful answers.

Financial Participation

Finally, if the church deems the missionary candidate qualified and acceptable, how can it become actively involved in supporting the missionary candidate financially? Should the missionary be just a name on a financial statement or prayer sheet? If not, how can the missionary truly become an extension of his supporting church? The Philippian model was searched for answers to these questions.

The Philippian model describes at length the financial role the local church can play in the ministry of its missionaries (Philippians 4:1-23). The church that is meticulous in its scrutiny must be prepared to be sacrificial in its giving. Why is a missionary made to go through an exhaustive and intensive interview process for a paltry sum of money? The Philippian model describes the financial participation that the local church should have in the lives of worthy candidates.

Thus the book of Philippians was observed to collect data on Paul's attitudes and opinions regarding interpersonal relationships, surrender and commitment, prayer, contentment, preaching, vision, education, separation, and finances. Each topic is described at length as a separate chapter in this book.

Delimitations

Once an instrument was developed from the book of Philippians for the local church to use in evaluating missionary candidates, it was sent to several major educators and administrators from Baptist mission boards for their evaluation. Of necessity, the author established several delimitations.

Confinement to the Book of Philippians

In finding an alternative to the Pauline model in the book of Acts, the author limited his study to the book of Philippians, even though Paul wrote letters to other churches that he had established. The epistles to the Corinthians, however, concentrate more on church order, while the epistles to the Thessalonians concentrate on eschatological issues. The book of Philippians, on the other hand, is written largely to thank the Philippian believers for their financial missionary support. Thus, the focus of the book is more missions-oriented. This is not to say that missiological helps cannot be found in other works. It is to say that the author believes that more straightforward help can be found in the book of Philippians.

Confinement to Baptist Mission Agencies

Why did the author purposely send this instrument to only people of Baptist belief and practice? This was done because the instrument was designed for Baptist churches. Certainly those of other denominations are doing significant mission work around the world for the glory of God. The local Baptist church, however, has a limited number of dollars to contribute to the cause of world evangelism.

These dollars should be invested in individuals who will reproduce similar churches on the mission field. This demands limiting one's funds to missionaries of similar Baptist persuasion. Therefore, the author sought only the opinion of Baptist mission executives.

Limitations

As the instrument was being prepared, the author attempted to avoid unnecessary confusion and difficulty. Still certain limitations must be expected.

Erroneous Hermeneutic

No single interpreter is infallible in his approach to the Scripture. Certainly this author has errors in his theology, but he does not know where they are. If he knew where they were, he would change his views. This human fallibility means that the interpretation of the book of Philippians is subject to error. This potential problem was addressed in the evaluation of the missionary executives. It is possible, however, that the executives have the same biases as the developer of the instrument. To the degree that this occurred, the study is limited.

Untruthful Evaluations

Each missionary executive who was asked to do an evaluation received a questionnaire that was supplied by the author. This questionnaire was developed with the help of the Temple Baptist Seminary faculty who are gifted in this particular area. The danger exists, however, that those who received the questionnaire did not answer truthfully. Friendliness towards the seminary or the author may have caused certain executives to be less than honest in their critiques. To the degree that this happened, the study is limited.

Assumptions

For a study of this type to take place, several presuppositions must be accepted as true. These assumptions are listed below.

The Bible Is the Word of God

Because the goal was to find a reliable instrument to evaluate missionary candidates, the Word of God was the author's source for principles and standards. The evaluation of the instrument by experienced mission executives guaranteed that the author interpreted the Word of God correctly. To the degree that the author has properly interpreted Scripture, his instrument is correct, even though it may have found opposition from the evaluators. In the final analysis, the Word of God sits in judgment on the evaluators, not the evaluators on the Word of God. If the evaluators had difficulty with the instrument, they were asked to show a Biblical justification for their difficulties. The underlying assumption was always present that the Bible is the Word of God.

Baptist Polity Is Preferable

Some may argue with the development of this instrument because its scope is limited to those of a Baptist persuasion. Indeed, the debate over polity issues is significant and must be entertained in a church-planting situation. Such debates, however, do not fall within the scope of this study. Because the researcher is a Baptist, and those who are asked to evaluate the instrument are Baptists, it is assumed that Baptist policy is best.

Local Churches Are Accountable

Some may object to the entire idea of churches scrutinizing missionary candidates with such care. After all, is not the mission board doing this in candidate school? Are not mission boards better prepared to do this than local churches? Who is the local church to turn down a candidate who has been found worthy by a respectable mission organization? Unfortunately, such thinking is not uncommon. Though many give token assent to the importance of the local church in missions, many mission boards desire the local church's financial support, but not its input. This study assumes that the local church not only has the right, but also the responsibility to evaluate carefully the missionary candidates who come before it for support. A church should be no less careful in choosing its missionaries than in choosing its pastor.

Definition of Terms

To better understand the scope of the research that has been undertaken several key terms must be defined. The following terms demand clarification.

Prayer Letter

The term *prayer letter* refers to the correspondence that a supporting church receives from one of its missionaries. This correspondence is called a *prayer letter* because it often contains requests for prayer. The prayer letter, however, is not limited to prayer requests. It updates the supporting church on the missionary himself and the work that he is conducting. Paul's letter to the Philippian church is a prayer letter.

Missionary

The term *missionary* is not found in the Bible. George Peters states that the word "comes from the Latin word *mitto*— 'I send' —and thus is closely related to the New Testament *apostello*— 'to send.'"[8] From Paul's words in I Corinthians 9:1-2, however, it would appear that a necessary qualification of an apostle was to have seen the risen Lord and to have been sent out by Him. It should be noted also that, according to Acts 1:21-22, the apostles gave definite witness to the facts of the ministry of Jesus and to His resurrection.

The ministry of the apostles, therefore, ceased with the passing of the first generation Christians. The foundational ministry of prophets also ceased (Ephesians 2:20). Thus, the only offices now in place in God's plan for advancement are evangelists and pastor-teachers (Ephesians 4:11).

Since the apostles and prophets were foundational and have passed from the scene, Ephesians 4:11-12 is probably meant to show a progression of development toward maturity. If the apostles and prophets laid the foundation for the church, and if the pastor-teacher assumes an established church and brings that church along in spiritual development, then the assumption may be made that the evangelist is one who plants the church upon the foundation that was laid by the apostles and prophets. New Testament evangelists were church planters; they were the "rank and file" missionaries of the church.

---

[8]George W. Peters, A Biblical Theology of Missions (Chicago: Moody Press, 1972), 249.

Missionaries then, as this paper uses the term, refers to those who have been called by God to evangelize the lost, disciple those converted, and organize local churches. The missionary, in turn, trains nationals to pastor the churches that have been planted.

Candidate

The term *candidate* refers to the missionary who is in the process of raising funds to go to the mission field. As a *candidate*, the missionary usually travels from church to church presenting his prospective field of service.

Pre-field Ministry

Pre-field ministry, commonly called "deputation," involves traveling from church to church and presenting the work to which the missionary feels called. The church then decides whether it desires to participate financially in this work. This paper is designed to help the church in this decision-making process.

Significance of the Study

In addition to developing an instrument from the book of Philippians and having it evaluated by missionary executives, the author desires to make a significant contribution to the sphere of missiology. This desire encompasses three broad areas.

A Missiological Commentary on Philippians

The book of Philippians is often approached from a psychological perspective. Indeed, many commentators have argued that the major theme of Philippians is being joyful. While no one can dispute that joy is a major theme

26

of the book, it must never be forgotten that the work is primarily a missionary prayer letter. The inspiration of the Holy Spirit certainly raises the level of this correspondence above that of an ordinary missionary letter, but a prayer letter it is nonetheless. Often this feature of the letter is ignored or relegated to secondary consideration. In so doing, a major contribution to the field of missions has been overlooked. The author has commented on this prayer letter as a prayer letter.

An Aid to Local Churches

Often the only criterion used by the local church to select its missionaries is the candidate's participation in an approved mission agency. This creates problems in that mission boards are not of Biblical origin. This is not to say that a mission board cannot be a valuable asset to the local church. The local church, however, is the only God-ordained institution for sending missionaries. The local church should not abdicate to a mission board the responsibility entrusted to it by God. The author desires to be a significant help to local churches by providing them with Biblical tools for making evaluations that God has given them to make.

An Aid to Missionary Candidates

The missionary candidate is often prepared by his Bible college or seminary to have a Biblical philosophy of ministry. Pastors, however, have often found that men who were prepared philosophically were not prepared personally. It is desired that this study will be a significant help to those who are called to the mission field, not in the sense of strengthening their beliefs or philosophies, but in the sense of strengthening them personally. The candidate who is all that he can be spiritually no doubt will last on the field when others have "packed it in" and gone home.

Chapter 2
Interpersonal Relationships

Thomas Hale boldly states that interpersonal conflict is "the number-one cause of missionaries leaving the field earlier than planned."[9] Many missionaries who possess a flawless philosophy of missions struggle in the area of interpersonal relationships. Even the Apostle Paul had to separate from Barnabas because "the contention" over John Mark "was so sharp between them" (Acts 15:39). Nevertheless, Paul recognized the value of interpersonal relationships and sought at the end of his life to rectify the division (2 Timothy 4:11).

In the opening verses of Philippians (1:1-2), Paul presents four interpersonal relationships that are necessary for the missionary. These include a relationship with Christ, fellow workers, nationals, and supporting churches.

A Relationship With Christ

The president of Asbury College, Dennis Kinlaw, tells the story of a man who quit his university studies, sold his possessions, and bought a one-way ticket to Latin America to serve as a missionary among a primitive tribe of Indians. The family of this 20-year-old had opposed his departure. The young man had no financial backing. Yet at the time of the story, this missionary had been working with these Indians for over ten years. When asked why he had gone when he did, the young man replied that he had

---

[9]Thomas Hale, <u>On Being a Missionary</u> (Pasadena, CA: William Carey Library, 1995), 171.

an intimacy with Jesus that would be lost if he were disobedient.[10]

The greatest credential any missionary can carry to the field is an intimacy with Jesus Christ. "The spiritual life of the missionary is basic to the success of a missionary career."[11] The relationship that the missionary has with Jesus must be nurtured at all costs. This is especially true on the mission field where there are "fewer props, fewer supports, fewer opportunities for fellowship, where the church may be small and weak, and the language hard to understand."[12] The missionary's ultimate support comes from his relationship with Christ.

Missionaries will constantly be tempted to allow the work of ministry to take precedence over a personal relationship with Jesus Christ. Spiritual barrenness, however, will be alleviated if the missionary spends adequate time developing his love relationship with God. Time must be spent with Jesus, for spirituality grows out of that intimacy.

---

[10]Hale, 331.

[11]Joel S. Lunde, "Curriculum Proposals in Mission for the Lutheran Brethren Seminary" (D.Miss. diss., Trinity Evangelical Divinity School, 1985), 106.

[12]Hale, 331-32.

This, of course, implies personal conversion. "A person who is sent forth as a missionary is a person who must be converted."[13] The opening confession of Paul, that he was a servant of Jesus Christ (1:1), shapes the entire book of Philippians. Paul was keenly aware of that day on the Damascus Road when Christ arrested him (3:12). Since then Paul had been the slave of Jesus, and this conviction shaped Paul's entire missionary endeavor. "The missionary who is not sure of his own salvation is not likely to lead others to a saving knowledge of Christ."[14]

In New Testament times, millions of slaves populated the Roman Empire. The vast majority of these were forced into slavery and kept there by legislation. While some of the more educated and skilled slaves held significant positions, most slaves were treated as the personal property of the owner. They were considered little better than work animals. These slaves had no right under the law and could even be killed with impunity by their masters.[15] When, therefore, Paul calls himself and Timothy "servants of Jesus Christ," he means that they are to be considered slaves in the most unassuming sense. Because of his love for the Lord, Paul was completely at Christ's disposal. His relationship to Christ took precedence over everything else. He was the bond slave of Jesus Christ.

---

[13]William B. Park, "The Strategy for Local Church Missions" (D.Min. diss., Faith Theological Seminary, 1983), 55.

[14]Herbert J. Kane, The Making of a Missionary (Grand Rapids: Baker Book House, 1975), 68.

[15]John F. MacArthur, Jr., Romans 1-8 (Chicago: Moody Press, 1991), 5.

A proper relationship with the Lord is the fountain from which other good interpersonal relationships flow. "Once a person has the right relationship to the Lord, he will very likely have the ability to get along with family, friends, pastors, deacons, church members, fellow missionaries and anyone else that he bumps shoulders with on a day-to-day basis."[16] The grace that is needed when others become irritable, and the peace that is needed when one is tempted to become irritable himself, both stem from one's relationship with God. As Paul clearly states, both "grace" and "peace" come "from God our Father, and from the Lord Jesus Christ" (1:2). Thus, one's relationship with God takes precedence over all other relationships, because it is this relationship that provides the spiritual enablement needed to deal with others.

A Relationship With Fellow Workers

Virtually all mission work is done in teams. Jesus sent out His disciples two by two. There is wisdom in this. Solomon said, "Two are better than one because they have a good reward for their labor" (Ecclesiastes 4:9). It is not surprising, therefore, to see Paul frequently paired with a fellow worker, in this case Timothy.

Because Paul was conscious of Timothy's unique gifts, it was fitting that Paul should choose him as a companion and fellow worker (Romans 16:21). Later in the book of Philippians Paul would describe the relationship between himself and Timothy in terms of a father-son relationship (2:22). Timothy became an indispensable partner to the Apostle Paul (Acts 17:14-15).[17]

---

[16]Park, 79.

[17]Herbert Lockyer, <u>All the Men of the Bible</u> (Grand Rapids: Zondervan Publishing House, 1958), 329.

Unfortunately, many missionaries never experience this kind of partnership with their colleagues. Ronald Iwasko lists "interrelationships with other missionaries" as a significant pressure of first-term missionaries,[18] while Hale points out, "Three quarters of all significant problems a missionary confronts are caused by relationship difficulties with other missionaries."[19] In light of these facts, local churches must be concerned about how well prospective missionary candidates relate to others. The inability to get along will be magnified on the mission field by "the high level of stress and frustration missionaries face and by the closeness of their living and working conditions."[20] Historically missionaries are strong-willed people. Therefore, they must intentionally seek to prevent interpersonal conflicts, especially among fellow workers.

Relationship problems with nationals do exist, but these are not nearly as intense as those between missionaries. Most missionaries are mentally prepared for differences with nationals, but they do not expect to have such strong disagreements with their fellow missionaries. [21]

"Rubbing people the wrong way" is a greater danger on the mission field because missionaries have to live in close quarters. Some of them live on compounds where

---

[18]Ronald Iwasko, "A Personnel Director Speaks to Professors of Mission," paper delivered at the Evangelical Theological Society, 42nd National Conference, New Orleans, LA, 15-17 November 1990.

[19]Hale, 40.

[20]Hale, 40.

[21]Hale, 172.

they are around other missionaries 12 or more hours a day, 7 days a week. If one person in this group is abrasive, life for the others can be miserable. "Nowhere are interpersonal relations more important than on the mission field."[22]

Self-assertiveness frequently manifests itself as missionaries try to get their own way. Such assertiveness may indicate that the missionary is placing a higher value on his own beliefs and objectives than on those of his fellow workers. He can quickly sacrifice the interests of other missionaries in order to protect his own interests. This is detrimental to camaraderie on the field.[23]

Jealously is also a great hindrance on the field. Those who are slow to learn the language may become jealous of those who are quick to learn it. Those who are not appointed to leadership positions become jealous of those who are. Those who are not respected by the nationals become jealous of those who are. When a missionary is jealous, he often desires to tear others down. Resentment and gossip are frequent occurrences. These problems can destroy team unity.[24]

Unity among missionary workers cannot be stressed too frequently. Divided workers are both weakened and neutralized. One of Satan's most effective tactics is to divide missionary workers through interpersonal conflict. It is therefore important that missionaries take practical steps to make their teams more harmonious and efficient.

---

[22]Hale, 62.

[23]Hale, 174.

[24]Hale, 175.

Thomas Hale suggests six steps to achieve this. First, most teams do better with someone assigned as a leader. The second thing that is necessary for the effective functioning of a team is that the team members submit to their leader. Third, all members of the team must be personally committed to each other. In addition, the basic goals of the group must be shared by all. The fifth thing necessary for an effective team is that each member recognizes and values the strengths of the others. Finally, prayer is necessary for team effectiveness.[25]

The missionary is a member of a team, and he must learn to be a harmonious worker. There are too many jobs to be done and too many roles to be filled for him to be a loner. He must be willing to "step up" and do a job, not thinking of self-interest.[26] As Paul told the Philippians, "Let nothing be done through strife or vainglory, but in lowliness of mind let each esteem others better than themselves. Look not every man on his own things, but every man also on the things of others" (2:3-4). This admonition was even more powerful because the Philippians had seen the way Paul and Timothy applied these principles as they related to each other. "Paul always worked with friends and kept his associates close to him."[27]

Timothy evidently became a Christian on Paul's first visit to Lystra (I Corinthians 4:17). He was the son of a

---

[25]Hale, 218-20.

[26]Hale, 63-64.

[27]Dean S. Gilliland, Pauline Theology and Mission Practice (Grand Rapids: Baker Book House, 1983), 277.

Jewess who had also become a Christian. Timothy's father, however, was a Greek, and the Biblical text suggests that he was dead and that he had not been a Christian (Acts 16:1). Paul's attention was drawn to Timothy because of a good report given of him by the local Christians. Paul wished to have Timothy as a companion in his ministry work (Acts 16:2).

There was, however, one problem. Timothy was the product of a mixed marriage. Jews were not supposed to marry Gentiles, but when this happened, the children were supposed to be regarded as Jewish. This had not taken place in the case of Timothy, for he had not been circumcised. His mother may not have taken her Jewish responsibility seriously, or the father may have refused to sanction the circumcision. Whatever the case, because Paul's ministry would bring Timothy in close contact with Jewish people, and it was well known in the area that Timothy had not been circumcised, Paul took the necessary step (Acts 16:3).

Timothy was qualified to be called a Jew, but because of his mother's mixed marriage he may have been considered illegitimate. Jewish opinion was divided as to whether the children of a mixed marriage were legitimate or illegitimate. It was necessary, therefore, to help Timothy gain credibility in the eyes of the Jews among whom he would be working.[28]

Paul could have been tempted to forego the circumcision, having just completed the Jerusalem Council where

---

[28]I. Howard Marshall, The Acts of the Apostles (Grand Rapids: Eerdmans Publishing Company, 1980), 259-60.

he vehemently argued that circumcision had nothing to do with the Gospel. Timothy could also have refused the circumcision in order to honor his father, but both men placed their personal feelings aside. They performed the circumcision, and a beautiful ministry team was formed. The words "Paul and Timothy" (1:1) very strongly communicated to the believers at Philippi a strong interpersonal relationship between fellow missionary laborers.

A Relationship With Nationals

In addition to a relationship with Christ and fellow workers, the Apostle Paul always had a vibrant relationship with those to whom he had come to minister. His correspondence to the Philippian church reveals the nature of his heart. It was unthinkable to the Apostle Paul to neglect "all the saints which are at Philippi in Christ Jesus" (1:1). This comprehensive phrase describes "the Christian community which had been formed following the apostolic mission at Philippi."[29]

The establishment of the church at Philippi marked the entrance of the Gospel into Europe. The narrative in Acts bears witness to the presence of a Jewish community before the arrival of the Christian missionaries (Acts 16:13). It was to a group of Jewish women that Paul first addressed his message, and this resulted in the conversion of Lydia. The remaining verses in Acts 16, however, make it clear that the Gospel was not restricted to Jews. A slave girl and a Roman jailer were both converted out of paganism.[30] Paul, therefore, had to know something about

---

[29]Ralph P. Martin, The Epistle of Paul to the Philippians (Grand Rapids: Eerdmans Publishing Company, 1987), 58.

relationships with those of varying ethnic and cultural backgrounds.

"Over the past three centuries, one of the most crucial and frequently debated issues in missions has had to do with the relationships between missionaries and nationals."[31] Because the modern missionary movement began during the time of colonial expansion, missionaries often copied the practices of Western administration. Consequently, many nationals were treated as uncivilized subordinates. Local people were denied access into the homes of missionaries. The missionary and the "native" would not drink from the same cup during the Lord's Supper. Unfortunately, many of these same prejudices still exist. As Salamone has rightly observed, however, missionaries should demonstrate "more real ethnological concern" than ethnologists.[33]

Many missionaries are convinced that Western culture is superior. The words "Christianity" and "civilization" are almost used interchangeably. If the missionary is not careful, he can easily reveal a superiority complex to the nationals he is attempting to evangelize. Local products are constantly compared unfavorably to those available in the states. Indeed, many missionaries arrive on the field with two dozen drums of personal items. This all conveys to the national that American goods are superior to their

---

[31]Paul Hiebert, Anthropological Insights for Missionaries (Grand Rapids: Baker Book House, 1987), 248.

[32]Hiebert, 248-49.

[33]Frank A. Salamone, ed., Anthropologists and Missionaries, studies in third world societies (Williamsburg: College of William and Mary, 1985).

goods. The only reason the missionary has gone to all the trouble and expense to ship these items is because he believes American goods are better in craftsmanship, quality, and durability. The national sees all of this as nothing short of bigotry.[34]

Hiebert points out that the missionary must "from the very first day" develop meaningful relationships with local people.[35] This is apparently what Paul did with the Philippians (4:5). When one enters a new culture, he should communicate his need for help and his desire to learn. When the missionary enters another culture as a genuine student, nationals are usually able to teach, for they are proud of their culture. While the culture is being absorbed, the missionary is able to build relationships that make him a part of the community. Learning the new culture also provides a significant opportunity to evangelize. Opportunities for witness are discovered when the missionary enters the culture as a student. The nationals do not view students as a threat.[36]

The missionary must also learn to love nationals as they are. At first this may be hard to do, in part because they seem so different from us. The missionary must do his best, however, not to place the national's culture in an unfavorable light compared to his own culture.[37] On a recent mission trip to the Dominican Republic, a Dominican auto mechanic who had promised a car in four hours, but had not completed his work in four days, frustrated a visiting pastor. He disdainfully asked the missionary why

---

[35]Hiebert, 82.

[36]Hiebert, 82.

[37]Hiebert, 84.

he continued to put up with this cultural failure to recognize time. The missionary responded that he was very close to leading the mechanic to Christ, and the pastor felt very guilty about seeing the man's cultural "shortcomings" rather than his eternal soul. The missionary must view himself culturally as an equal of, rather than a superior to, the national. "When people engage in relationships with people of the same category, they feel secure and expect to benefit. However, when people relate across structure, they anticipate danger or even disaster."[38]

Love must be the hallmark of the missionary. Jesus came as a missionary from heaven to express the Father's love. In a similar way, the modern missionary also goes into the world to express the Father's love. "Missionaries do not have to be bright or brave to be successful (though both are very desirable), but they must be loving. The nationals will overlook many weaknesses and forgive many blunders if they are persuaded that the missionary has a heart of love."[39] Marjorie Collins is correct when she states, "Placement of a verb, or the wrong gender of a noun will matter little if there is a recognizable love and respect for those among whom" the missionary works.[40]

In addition, if missionaries hope to be effective in managing conflict in another culture, they must learn to adapt their approaches and expectations to fit that culture. Nationals frequently consider flexibility to be an important

---

[38]Sherwood Lingenfelter, Agents of Transformation (Grand Rapids: Baker Book House, 1996), 192.

[39]Kane, 70.

[40]Marjorie Collins, Manual for Today's Missionary (Pasadena, CA: William Carey Library, 1986), 184.

trait of the missionary. "Missionaries who are rigid in following their own cultural ways and who refuse to adapt and fit into the host culture are not greatly appreciated."[41]

This is true even after nationals have been saved and incorporated into the church. Missionaries frequently criticize young national churches. Attitudes and behaviors are uncharitably and judgmentally dissected. In the course of criticizing the national leadership, however, the missionary discourages and impedes church growth. Many times the missionary does this because he wants to keep control of the church. Such slander, however, tears Christians apart and encourages the nationals to slander each other.[42]

Paul, in contrast, viewed the Philippian believers as fellow saints (1:1). He treated them as brothers rather than children. By the time of the Philippian correspondence, the young church had already become dependent upon the Holy Spirit and independent of the personality of Paul. Indeed, Paul was receiving support from them, rather than vice versa.

The Philippian church, despite its young age, was a mighty instrument for the conversion of others. It had developed significantly, in spite of the fact that its first three converts were a female merchant, a demon-possessed slave girl, and a suicidal jailer. Look at what God accomplished through this assembly! While it is true that

---

[41]Donald C. Palmer, "Development of a Manual on Conflict Management for Training GMU Missionaries" (D.Min. diss., Trinity Evangelical Divinity School, 1990), 90.

[42]Hale, 128.

Missionaries have the responsibility to teach, admonish, and equip the membership of the young national church, they also need to respect what God can do independently of them in the lives of these new stumbling believers.[43]

In addition, the nationals are the only ones who have some degree of permanence in the area. Many missionaries, like Paul, are transients; they do not have local roots. Missionaries need to entrust the communication of the Gospel to those who will be most effective in doing so. Nationals also keep the church from appearing foreign. According to Hale, national leadership enhances growth more often than it hinders the church; thus, the missionary should seek to take a back seat.[44] Missionaries should seek to be servants and supporters of the church, viewing themselves as partners with the nationals.[45]

Often the two major areas of relational difficulty for missionaries are managing conflict and communicating cross-culturally. These two problem areas merge together when proper relationships are not established with the nationals. It is the job of the missionary to ensure that mutual understanding is taking place.[46]

A Relationship With Supporting Churches

Once nationals have been saved, they need to be congregated into a local church. While some have fought

---

[43]Hale, 129.

[44]Hale, 127-28.

[45]Hale, 126.

[46]Palmer, 76, 92.

against any formal church organization, believing that the church is merely a spiritual organization, the New Testament gives clear evidence of a definitely organized church. The first church in Jerusalem knew the number of its members, united in worship services and prayer meetings, and observed the ordinances. As this early church progressed, a formal church organization developed. Meetings were held on the first day of the week, and church decorum was practiced.[47]

In addition, the early church had offices of elders and deacons. On his first missionary journey, Paul ordained elders in every church (Acts 14:23). The permanent nature of the offices of elder and deacon are evident by the list of qualifications given in the Pastoral Epistles (I Timothy 3; Titus 1:5-9). It is not surprising, therefore, to find the Philippian letter addressed to the saints "with the bishops and deacons" (1:1).[48] "The terms refer to the inner life of the church as an organized fellowship."[49]

The duty of the bishops is clearly revealed in Acts 20:28 where the word is translated "overseers." These leaders are responsible for nourishing and protecting the flock of God.[50]

Deacons, on the other hand, took their name from those in the secular world who were responsible for certain

---

[47]Robert L. Saucy, The Church in God's Program (Chicago: Moody Press, 1972), 98-99.

[48]Saucy, 99.

[49]Martin, 58.

[50]Martin, 59.

welfare duties in the community.[51] When the term was used in Greek prose, it usually denoted a servant within the household whose duties consisted of waiting on tables and doing marketing for the household. Since the Philippian letter was written to thank the church for its contribution to missions, "it is possible to see the bishops and deacons mentioned as the organizers of that collection, with the deacons assisting the bishops in the actual work of overseeing the collection."[52] New Testament evidence seems to indicate that deacons were primarily concerned with the material ministries of the church.

All of this indicates that the missionary work of the Apostle Paul in Philippi culminated with the planting of an organized local church. This church eventually became a source of support for the Apostle Paul's missionary endeavors. Paul is writing back to this church and its leadership to thank them for their contributions. Thus, the Apostle Paul not only had a relationship with Christ, his fellow workers, and the nationals with whom he ministered, but he also had a relationship with the local churches that supported him with financial gifts and prayers.

"A missionary learns right away that reports must be made to all who contribute to his work."[53] While it is true that keeping the supporting brethren informed is a monumental task, it must be done. Are modern missionaries

---

[51]Martin, 59.

[52]Saucy, 153, 156.

[53]Joseph L. Cannon, For Missionaries Only (Grand Rapids: Baker Book House, 1969), 42.

busier than the Apostle Paul who took the time to write this beautiful piece of correspondence?

As soon as a missionary is notified of a gift in his account, he should write a note of thanks to the donor. A friendly word of genuine thanks and the certain knowledge that he appreciates the gift will establish true Christian fellowship and friendship with those who make it possible for him to serve. Local churches are under no obligation to continue support indefinitely, and the more the missionary does to show his sincere appreciation, the more interested that local church will be in caring for his needs. The local church supports the missionary because it has confidence in him as a missionary and considers his support a wise investment. The missionary must encourage supporters to continue to feel that he is worthy of this interest.[54]

The missionary must also sense a certain amount of accountability to those from whom he receives contributions. The Holy Spirit sends out missionaries through the agency of the local church (Acts 13:1-4). Many local churches cannot easily maintain and supervise their missionaries on the field without the help of a mission board, but this in no way releases the missionary from being accountable to the local church. All missionaries must answer to local churches, especially those from whom they receive financial support.[55] The relationship between a missionary and his supporting churches must remain a priority.

---

[54]Collins, 106.

[55]Hale, 49.

A Summary Application for the Local Church

Without the ability to maintain good interpersonal relationships the missionary "with impeccable ministry credentials will not have a satisfactory ministry experience in the new cultural environment."[56] It, therefore, becomes imperative for the local church, when analyzing a prospective missionary, to evaluate his relationship to Christ, fellow workers, nationals, and supporting churches.

Many mission boards have elaborate administrative procedures to identify interpersonal conflict in its infancy. They also have developed procedures to prevent its occurrence. Annual reports and evaluations, meetings at various times throughout the year, scheduled interviews, as well as workers' conferences have all been used. Moreover, personnel such as administrators, project leaders, counselors, and speakers have all been used to lecture on these topics. Procedures, however, as beneficial as they can be, rarely prevent interpersonal conflict. There is no substitute for communication.[57]

The only way to evaluate effectively the interpersonal skill of the missionary candidate is to spend time with him in prolonged conversation. For example, recently I met with a missionary candidate who had an excellent philosophy of ministry. The introductory packet that he sent to the church flawlessly presented a Biblical approach to missions. The college from which he graduated was a

---

[56]Nancy N. Palmer, "Cross Cultural Training and Orientation for Missionaries with Special Reference to the North American Baptist Conference" (M.A. diss., Nazarene Theological Seminary, 1987), 21.

[57]Hale, 205.

solid fundamental school, and he had selected a well-respected mission board. As pastor, I would have recommended that our congregation financially participate in his ministry—that is, until I ate with this missionary. During the course of our meal, he criticized the food and the service, other churches that he had visited, his wife, his mission board, his pastor, and a host of other things. It was obvious that this missionary had some deep-seated resentment that needed to be addressed. He did not have a good relationship with his Lord, his fellow workers, his target audience, or his supporting churches. Until these interpersonal conflicts were resolved, he was doomed to fail.

I challenged this missionary candidate about these things, because "the time for personal assessment in these areas is before moving to a new culture. One should not wait until experiencing the stress of learning a new culture, language, and job to try to improve" his ability to work harmoniously with others.[58]

Indeed, it will be difficult for the missionary candidate to raise support if he appears to be resentful of others. "Most conflicts between people are not one-time occurrences."[59] The prospective supporting church should not, therefore, excuse poor interpersonal relationships as trivial. Instead, "the missionary candidate should be challenged to make managing conflict an important goal of his life. This will outweigh any one particular issue since a healthy relationship is necessary for long-term effectiveness."[60]

---

[58]Nancy Palmer, 23.

[59]Donald Palmer, 95.

[60]Donald Palmer, 95.

Another missionary candidate introduced to this author has been on deputation for several years, yet he has raised only a very small percentage of his needed missionary support. This missionary candidate has been in numerous churches; contacts are not his problem. When he enters these churches, however, he proceeds to tell the various pastors all that is wrong in the other churches he has previously visited. The pastor cannot help but feel that he will be the latest addition to this missionary's scandal sheet. Is it any wonder this missionary is struggling to raise support? Perhaps the churches of America are saving the heathen from a missionary who will hinder, rather than help, the cause of Christ.

Chapter 3
Surrender and Commitment

Many Christians have witnessed young people who have surrendered their lives for full-time missionary service. Tragically, however, few of these ever make it to the mission field. The fervor that was felt in the youth rally, camp, or evangelistic meeting quickly wanes. Ironically, as I was doing the research for this chapter, a couple in our church called the office and asked to take me out to lunch. Their concern was that their daughter had surrendered to go to the mission field, but over the past years at our church they had seen too many people surrender to go and then drop out.

This type of drop-out is far more serious than the high school drop-out. The student who drops out of high school will find it difficult to secure profitable employment, but the missionary drop-out will effect the eternal well-being of perhaps hundreds of other people. His failure to go with the Gospel to the lost world will result in irreparable consequences.[61]

Dowdy estimates that only one out of every fifty young people who volunteer for full-time missionary service make it to the field.[62] Dowdy suggests fourteen reasons why this is true, and most of these revolve around the surrender and commitment level of the volunteer. These include improper understanding of commitment, fear of personal sacrifice, a failure to see missionaries who are

---

[61]J. Paul Dowdy, "The Problem of Missionary Volunteer Drop-Outs," Grace Journal 7 (1966), 22.

[62]Dowdy, 23.

thrilled and excited about their work, lack of constant encouragement from pastors and families, the attraction of more profitable and less taxing work, lack of initiative, a realization that their call to missions was a mistake on their part, and an unwillingness of parents to have them go to the mission field.[63] Many of these reasons suggest that the missionary volunteer is not fully surrendered or does not have a strong enough commitment to make it.

Problems with surrender and commitment do not get better once a missionary makes it to the field. "A person may have come out planning to spend two or three terms on the field, but leaves after one."[64] Many missionaries arrive on the field intending to stay as long as the Lord wills. When they decide to leave for whatever reason, they will say they are following God's leading. In some cases this is so, but in many cases it is not. Self-deception is easy to do. Some missionaries choose the mission field as if they were choosing a career or a company. If things do not work out, they leave.

Hale lists some of the common reasons why missionaries drop out: health reasons, needs of aged parents at home, needs of children, job dissatisfaction, inability to adapt with resulting emotional distress, discouragement because of a lack of spiritual fruit, disagreement with mission policy and leadership decisions, concern for professional advancement, desire for the life at home, the wife's unhappiness after her children leave home, and psychological disorders. All these account for twenty-five percent of missionary drop-outs. The other seventy-five

---

[63]Dowdy, 24.

[64]Thomas Hale, On Being a Missionary (Pasadena, CA: William Carey Library, 1995), 326.

percent occur because of interpersonal conflicts with other missionaries.[65]

It would be helpful if the local church could know in advance which missionaries will "drop out" early. It is often these very missionaries who cause the greatest problems among their fellow workers. Unfortunately, there is no tool to identify these people. At best, the local church can detect special risk factors such as inflexibility, dogmatism, and an unwillingness to submit to authority. Such character traits indicate that the missionary "will not make a good adaptation to the mission field and hence will be more likely to drop out."[66]

Most missionaries, of course, will state that they are leaving the field for a good reason. Unfortunately, many of these justifications do nothing to help those who are left behind. Cannon states that there are "twice as many" missionaries "now residing at home as there [are] on the field."[67] The list of reasons for this is long, but "the reasons voiced and the actual cause can be two different things."[68] Could it be that many missionaries who have left the field for home are lacking in commitment and have failed to surrender? The very word "surrender" frightens people and has rather unfortunate connotations

---

[65]Hale, 327.

[66]Hale, 327.

[67]Joseph L. Cannon, <u>For Missionaries Only</u> (Grand Rapids: Baker Book House, 1969), 14.

[68]Cannon, 14.

of "conflict, crisis, and capitulation leading to a permanent subjugation."[69]

The Apostle Paul, however, had no such negative feelings. To him, surrender and commitment could be articulated with the word "confidence." Paul was confident that God would perform the work that He started. In the second major section of Philippians (1:3-7), the apostle presents four major things that contributed to this confidence, four things that triggered his surrender and commitment. These include an appreciative memory, an aggressive prayer life, an acknowledgment of God's sovereignty, and an emotional attachment to his converts.

An Appreciate Memory

Joseph Cannon states that he has "always admired the candor of the missionary who gave the real reason for leaving: 'I hate these people and can't stand them any longer.'"[70] One of the first challenges to the commitment level of the new missionary will be the shock that he faces upon entering a new culture. He will suddenly find himself unable to communicate, unable to understand the subtle cues that give meaning to life situations, and unable to understand the thought patterns of the new culture. He will suddenly be stripped of his natural leadership abilities. These factors tend to frustrate the new missionary and put him under heavy emotional strain. He may be unable to make the necessary adjustments to the culture in

---

[69]J. Herbert Kane, The Making of a Missionary (Grand Rapids: Baker Book House, 1975), 38.

[70]Cannon, 14-15.

order to continue work in the new environment in which he finds himself.[71]

It is imperative, therefore, that the missionary, from the very beginning, develop an appreciative love for the people he has been called to reach. The Apostle Paul had such an appreciative love. When he wrote back to the Philippian church, he could say, "I thank my God upon every remembrance of you" (1:3).

Memories are important things, and the Christian missionary must choose what he will remember and what he will forget. Later in the Philippian letter Paul said that he had forgotten those things that were behind (3:13). If the apostle was characterized by what he had forgotten, he was also characterized by what he had chosen to remember, and one thing he had chosen to remember with fondness was the Philippian believers. He had an appreciative memory with regard to them.

When the children of Israel left Egypt, they desired to return because they remembered the fish, cucumbers, melons, leeks, onions, and garlic of Egypt (Numbers 11:5). The Israelites, however, had forgotten the hard whip of the taskmaster. They had reason to return to Egypt because they remembered their time there in only a positive light, while judging their sojourn in the wilderness only in negative terms. In a similar manner, many missionaries upon arriving on the field, remember only good things about the United States while judging their new culture only in

---

[71]Harold R. Carpenter, "An Introduction to Assemblies of God Missions for Use at Central Bible College" (D.Miss. diss., Trinity Evangelical Divinity School, 1988), 164.

negative terms. This attitude is bound to ensure a quick return to the land from which they came.

Paul, on the other hand, remembered the Philippians, not in negative terms, but with positive memories. The apostle remembered the Philippians with warmth and had remained close to them over the years. This was due in part to the fact that Paul concentrated on their "fellowship in the Gospel" (1:5).

This phrase has been understood several ways. Some have taken the word κοινονια in a passive sense. The resulting phrase "your fellowship in the gospel" is taken to be equivalent to "your faith." According to this view, the word "gospel" references the content of the message that the Philippians had made their own at the first. There are better reasons, however, for understanding κοινονια in an active sense, denoting the Philippians' cooperation in the aid of the Gospel. This fits well with the other instances where the word "gospel" is used in this letter, where a good case can be made for taking the word in this dynamic sense. In addition, when Paul elsewhere uses the word κοινονια with the preposition εις, this active sense is apparent. Paul, then, gives thanks to God because the Philippians cooperated with him in his ministry of the Gospel to the Gentiles. The Philippians had been committed to this partnership in the gospel from the first day, that is, from the time of their conversion.[72] The translation "generosity" seems best to cover the apostle's thought as he thinks upon the way the church has supported him. The Philippian church had continued to show its interest in the Gospel by repeated contributions.

---

[72]Peter T. O'Brien, "The Fellowship Theme in Philippians," <u>Reformed Theological Review</u> 37, no. 1 (1978), 10-11.

The Philippian believers indicated the reality of their partnership in the Gospel by a keen activity in the interest of it.[73]

Phil Parshall states that emotional breakdowns have caused many missionaries to leave the field. According to his survey, a very large percentage of missionaries experience discouragement, and ninety-nine percent said that frustration was a part of their lives. It is not surprising, therefore, that ninety-seven percent of the missionaries surveyed said tension was an integral part of their lives. Twenty percent of the missionaries surveyed took tranquilizers, and twenty-six percent said that they drank occasionally.[74]

Does all of this suggest that many missionaries are focusing their attention on the wrong things? One of the marks of the natural man is an unthankful spirit (2 Timothy 3:2). The refusal to be thankful often results in feelings of discouragement and depression, which easily depletes the missionary's sense of surrender and commitment. Surrender and commitment are lost when an appreciative spirit is not maintained.

An Aggressive Prayer Life

Maintaining an appreciative spirit is not easy to do, but the Apostle Paul gives us a clue as to how this can be done when he writes, "Always in every prayer of mine for you all making request with joy" (1:4). Though some have seen this verse as an interruption between verses three and four, there is a direct correlation. It is difficult to maintain

---

[73]Ralph P. Martin, The Epistle of Paul to the Philippians (Grand Rapids: Eerdmans Publishing Company, 1987), 49, 62.

an attitude of appreciation toward those to whom one ministers when there is no prayer offered on their behalf. The missionary quickly finds his heart departing from the people for whom he has failed to pray.

Jesus told His followers to "pray for them that despitefully use you" (Matthew 5:44). Though the next chapter will be devoted entirely to the prayer life of the missionary, it must be pointed out here that the missionary's sense of surrender and commitment is directly related to his prayer life. The heart of the missionary will be removed from his target audience unless he habitually holds them up before the Throne of Grace. Even when the target audience treats the missionary with contempt, prayer can alleviate the sting. This is why Jesus told His followers to pray for those who are characterized by spite.

The Christian is to love his enemies. Jesus defines these "enemies" as those "who curse you" and "hate you" (Matthew 5:44). The missionary will be faced constantly with those who wish him evil and those who detest him. This often results in threats and insults, as well as physical violence. According to Christ, the proper answer to all this provocative and unprovoked treatment is love. The missionary is to respond with loving speech and kind actions. There is no way that the missionary can possess the grace to perform this apart from prayer.[75]

When I was in high school, the son of a missionary returned from Brazil to be educated in our Christian school. The first day this boy got on the bus, he made fun of my sister who had been born with a birth defect. I made up my mind right there that I did not like this boy. As God

---

[75]Guy H. King, New Order (Fort Washington, PA: Christian Literature Crusade, 1943), 62-63.

convicted my heart, however, I began to pray for him. Steadily, over time, this boy became one of my dearest friends in high school. When one prays for those who despitefully use him, he finds his heart turned toward those individuals.

If, therefore, the missionary is to stay on the field totally surrendered and committed to those to whom he is to minister, he must pray for them. This prayer must be like Paul's prayer — continual (the participle for "prayer" is present tense) and comprehensive ("for you all" embraces the whole fellowship of believers).[76] Surrender and commitment are tied to aggressive prayer.

An Acknowledgment of God's Sovereignty

In addition to an appreciative memory and an aggressive prayer life, the Apostle Paul was able to maintain high levels of surrender and commitment because he constantly acknowledged the sovereignty of God. Paul was able to look beyond the generosity of the Philippians to that work of grace within their lives that first gave them the impulse to contribute to his missionary labors. This redeeming and renewing work of God would continue to manifest itself "until the day of Jesus Christ" (1:6). Paul was confident that God's sovereignty would "preserve the community at Philippi in spite of its sufferings and in the face of assaults that were leveled against it."[77] This helped the apostle maintain a high level of commitment.

---

[76]Martin, 62.

[77]Martin, 63.

Thomas Hale is right when he asserts that when the missionary has thoughts of dropping out, his "first response must be to turn to God."[78] If the missionary has been wounded in the spiritual conflict, God has allowed these wounds. They are God's loving acts designed to help the missionary grow spiritually. Missionaries, however, like others, prefer to avoid such disciplines. The missionary can easily turn back from a life of self-denial and decide that the missionary life wasn't God's will for him after all.[79]

For the Christian, there is only one road to self-fulfillment, and that is by way of self-denial. "Call it 'unconditional surrender,' or just 'plain obedience,' or anything you wish; it doesn't make much difference."[80] The missionary must recognize that God is a sovereign God who allows certain things to happen in the life of His servants in order that He might perfect the good work that He has begun in them.

Much has been said about the hardships of missionary life. Consequently, the fear of failure is very real and acts as a strong deterrent. Through the years many young people have been kept from going into missionary work, and others have stopped once they have started, because of a sense of inadequacy. Paul, however, found the grace of God sufficient for every trial (2 Corinthians 12:9). The missionary must realize that he does not go out alone or in his own strength. Each one can say with David, "The Lord will perfect that which concerneth me" (Psalm

---

[78]Hale, 328.

[79]Hale, 328.

[80]Kane, 40.

138:8). If the missionary is a missionary by the will of God, he can be confident of spiritual success. It makes no difference whether he is learning a difficult language, adjusting to a strange culture, or living with difficult people, the grace of God can gird the missionary with tenacity to increase his surrender and commitment levels.[81]

Such faith demands a high view of God. J.I. Packer states that we are "poles apart" from our evangelical forefathers in this regard. Today, vast stress is placed on the thought that God is personal, and to a certain degree this limits God. It conveys the idea that God is weak, inadequate, and ineffective. Human beings are limited in space, in time, in knowledge, and in power, but God is not so limited. He is eternal, infinite, and almighty. Like man, God is personal, but unlike man, God is majestic. "In all its constant stress on the reality of God's personal concern for His people, and on the gentleness, tenderness, sympathy, patience, and yearning compassion that He shows towards them, the Bible never lets us lose sight of His majesty, and His unlimited dominion over His creatures."[82]

Unfortunately, the modern missionary has thoughts of God that are too human. In so doing, the missionary bears a resemblance to apostate Israel (Psalm 50:21). The missionary must never imagine that sentiment rather than principle moves God. He must never believe that Satan can thwart the designs of deity. God's plans and purposes are not constantly subject to change as we suppose. His

---

[81]Kane, 48-49.

[82]J.I. Packer, Knowing God (Downers Grove, IL: InterVarsity Press, 1973), 74.

power is not restricted.[83] God is able to complete that good work that He has begun, even when the missionary suspects that He is not able.

When the missionary is failing to acknowledge the sovereignty of God, there are two significant steps that he must take. The first is to remove from his thought limitations that would make God small. The second step is to look at the tasks that God has already done. When the missionary is despondent, cowed, and despairing, he must look at the good work that God has already accomplished.[84] In order to increase his faith that Christ will be able to complete His good work, the missionary must look at how that work has progressed since its beginning. The God who begins the work will finish the work.

The supremacy of God over the works of His hands is vividly depicted in the Bible. God divided the Red Sea, opened the earth to swallow rebels, and ordered the sun to stand still. At the sovereign command of God, ravens carried food; an iron floated on the water; lions became tame; and fire did not burn. "Whatsoever the Lord pleased, that did he in heaven, and in earth, in the seas, and all deep places" (Psalm 135:6). Nothing can thwart the sovereignty of God.[85]

Therefore, when the missionary has a desire to go home because of discouragement and the like, his problem largely stems from the fact that his God is too small. A

---

[83]Arthur W. Pink, Gleanings in the Godhead (Chicago: Mood Press, 1975), 28.

[84]Packer, 77.

[85]Pink, 30.

60

proper acknowledgment of the sovereignty of God always results in a heightened level of surrender and commitment.

An Emotional Attachment to One's Converts

A final thing that triggered the Apostle Paul's surrender and commitment was an emotional attachment to his converts. Paul had a continual thought for the people at Philippi, even though he was imprisoned (1:7).

When the Greek term ψρονειν is translated "thought," however, it does not give the full thrust of the original language. The word signifies a "sympathetic" interest and concern, expressing as it does the action of the heart as well as the intellect,"[86] Perhaps the best English word to render the thought is "concern." Paul was so concerned about his converts that he was vividly conscious of being present with them even when he was physically absent. This closeness was based on a common participation in the grace of God. A deep sense of oneness existed between them, even though the apostle and the church were separated by distance. This distance was further aggravated by the fact that Paul was "in bonds." Whether Paul was in prison or whether he was being arraigned before judges for the sake of the Gospel, the Phillippian believers and Paul were one.[87] This common participation in the grace of God gave Paul the strength he needed to remain completely surrendered and totally committed to his ministry.

Repeatedly in the Prison Epistles, Paul demonstrates an impressive belief in, and concern for, the develement

---

[86]Martin, 64.

[87]Martin, 64-65.

of his converts. Paul's aim was that the Philippians might progress in the faith (1:25). He was confident that God would continue the good work that He had begun in the Philippians (1:6). This desire for their well-being motivated Paul. When Paul thought of and prayed for the Philippians, he did so with joy (1:4) and thankfulness (1:3). The fact that Paul had the Philippian believers in his heart prevented the chains of imprisonment from being a source of discouragement. His ability to think of others, rather than himself, governed his levels of surrender and commitment.[88]

Nancy McCutcheon's research reveals that many prospective missionary candidates "have more of a 'what can I get' attitude, with a greater emphasis on meeting 'my needs.'"[89] Such missionaries have "trouble getting along with people and lack the ability to 'hang in there' when the going gets tough."[90] Thus, there is a direct correlation between selfishness and early departure. When the missionary holds in his heart his own personal feelings, rather than the interests of his converts, the likelihood exists that his surrender and commitment levels will not be very high.

Paul informed the Philippians that they were partakers with him of God's grace. These Christians were very dear

---

[88]Patrick Rogers, "Hopeful in Spite of Chains," Biblical Theology Bulletin 12, no. 3 (1982), 78-79.

[89]Nancy S. McCutcheon, "The Importance of Spiritual Psychological, Academic, and Skills Preparation for Missionary Candidates" (M.A. diss., Columbia Biblical Seminary, 1993), 57.

[90]McCutcheon, 57.

to the apostle, and this longing to be reunited with them was so great he could say he yearned for them with the very affection of Christ Himself.[91]

Any missionary who stays on the field does so not by his own diligence, but by God's grace. "When you take the mission out of the missionary he must pack up and leave."[92] When the grace of God is forgotten, the joy that comes from dedicated service is lost. When the missionary's heart does not perform as a participant in the grace of God, there will be no emotional attachment to his converts, and a missionary who is emotionally detached will soon find himself physically detached as well.

An Application to the Prospective Missionary

The answer to the alarming rise of missionary dropouts is not to warn missionary candidates that they may be making a mistake. In the local church's zeal to protect the mission field from misfits, it has effectively blocked many called and qualified people from entering the field. "The appeal should be made for missionary volunteers with the idea of encouraging them on to preparation, application, and finally to the field."[93]

Instead, the people in our churches who are alarmed at the astronomical number of missionary drop-outs should be challenged to encourage their friends on the field. This demands that our missionaries be challenged to have appreciative memories, aggressive prayer lives, frequent

---

[91]O'Brien, 12.

[92]Cannon, 15.

[93]Dowdy, 25.

acknowledgments of the sovereignty of God, and emotional attachment to their converts. Only then can the current lack of surrender and commitment be bolstered.

Whatever one does on the mission field will inevitably take more time and effort than a similar activity back home. Obstacles will abound, and discouragement will be battled constantly. Perseverance begins the day one arrives on the field (unless, of course, one considers that deputation demands perseverance too) and continues throughout the missionary's career. Perseverance demands endurance, "the willingness and capacity to suffer hardship, physical discomfort, opposition, and worse."[94] When it becomes evident that being a missionary is costly, nationals are able to see something that is worth many sermons. It is only as the missionary sacrifices and gives of himself that his witness becomes authentic.[95] All missionaries must say with the Apostle Paul, "We were willing to have imparted unto you, not the Gospel of God only, but also our own souls" (I Thessalonians 2:8).

---

[94]Hale, 39.

[95]Hale, 39.

Chapter 4
Prayer Life

How much time do missionaries actually spend in prayer? Phil Parshall discovered that eleven percent pray less than an average of five minutes a day, while sixty percent pray between eleven and thirty minutes daily. In addition, 257 of the missionaries surveyed said that they found their minds wandering during prayer, and only one respondent stated that this never happened to him. It is not surprising, therefore, to discover that 118 respondents identified the problem of maintaining a systematic devotional time as their greatest spiritual struggle. No other problem even came close to this one.[96]

Similarly, Nancy McCutcheon's research revealed that many missionaries were weak in their prayer lives. They doubted that God was able to accomplish His purposes through prayer and experienced a limited amount of specific answers to prayer. She stated, "Prospective missionaries seem to struggle to maintain a regular devotional life."[97]

Missionaries with their knowledge of psychology, anthropology, and sociology are tempted to lean on their own understanding (Proverbs 3:5) rather than look to the

---

[96]Phil Parshall, "How Spiritual Are Missionaries?" Evangelical Missions Quarterly 23, no. 1 (1987), 10-11.

[97]Nancy S. McCutcheon, "The Importance of Spiritual, Psychological, Academic, and Skills Preparation for Missionary Candidates" (M.A. diss., Columbia Biblical Seminary, 1993), 46.

Lord for His direction and guidance.[98] When I graduated from Bible College and was looking for a place of ministry, I fervently sent out résumés, made telephone calls, and put my name on placement lists in order to find a field of service. When nothing materialized right away, I went to the head of the Pastoral Studies Department and asked if there was anything else I could do. I will never forget his question to me. He asked, "You are praying, aren't you?" His question flooded my heart with conviction. Like every Christian, "prospective missionary candidates must realize the necessity and accept the responsibility personally for a daily devotional time with God."[99]

The prayer life of the missionary is very important. If this is neglected, the missionary places himself and his ministry in peril. There is no way that a missionary can be a man of God unless he systematically develops a time of daily prayer. On the mission field there are no large Christian communities or Bible colleges to buoy him up. Prayer meetings, chapel services, and dorm fellowships are all missing, and the missionary, humanly speaking, is on his own. He cannot depend upon others for growth and fellowship. "He must know how to cultivate his own spiritual life without any outside help."[100]

Most missionaries confess that this is one of their greatest problems. They are constantly ministering to others, and there is no one left to minister to them. If the missionary fails to guard zealously his quiet time alone

---

[98]Herbert J. Kane, The Making of a Missionary (Grand Rapids: Baker Book House, 1975), 55.

[99]McCutcheon, 49.

[100]Kane, 69.

66

with God, he will soon find himself robbed of both joy and power. Great missionaries of the past have testified to the importance of prayer in the missionary endeavor. It was said of Hudson Taylor during his fifty years in China, the sun never rose without finding him on his knees.[101]

Another great missionary who was characterized by prayer was the Apostle Paul. He frequently found himself in situations where his only recourse was prayer. One such instance is recorded in the Philippian correspondence (1:8-11). Paul had a heartfelt desire to see the Christians at Philippi, but this desire could not immediately be fulfilled in view of the apostle's imprisonment. This being the case, the only outlet that Paul had for his feelings was prayer, and the prayer recorded in the book of Philippians ranks among Paul's best. "Almost every word must be carefully weighed if the greatness and range of the petition are to yield their riches."[102] This prayer demonstrates two features that should be of vital interest to any prospective missionary. These are the purity of prayer and the purposes of prayer.

The Purity of Prayer

The first noticeable characteristic of Paul's prayer is that it stems from a pure heart. The apostle longed to be reunited with his converts, and this desire was so strong that it could be described as yearning with the heart of Jesus Himself (1:8), literally "in the entrails of Christ Jesus."

---

[101]Kane, 69.

[102]Ralph P. Martin, The Epistle of Paul to the Philippians (Grand Rapids: Eerdmans Publishing Company, 1987), 66.

In ancient thought, "the viscera were regarded as the seat of emotional life."[103] Paul had a pure love for his converts.

Anyone, however, can say that he has tender compassion. Paul, therefore, appeals to God. He asks the Lord to witness the veracity of his confession. Paul's prayer begins with God who knows the hearts of all men. This helps substantiate that the apostle is praying from motives that are pure.

Men are naturally and basically selfish. Christians in general and missionaries in particular, therefore, should examine their motives periodically, especially with regard to praying. One reason that missionaries experience spiritual poverty and powerlessness in prayer is a wrong motive (James 4:3). If one is carnal and desires material things merely to gratify the flesh, he cuts the lifeline of prayer. If Christians obey the exhortation of Matthew 6:33, they will pray only for those things that concern God's kingdom and God's glory. The self-seeking person fails to put God's glory first, and his requests are not granted. The missionary needs to be careful how he prays. Sincerity and a spirit of worship are insufficient to make a valid petition. Self-examination is very important, lest the missionary offer a prayer of pretense. It does not make sense to pray from a heart that is not pure before God.[104]

It is, therefore, imperative that the missionary practice the procedure of the Apostle Paul. Before talking to God,

---

[103]Martin, 66.

[104]Lehman Strauss, Sense and Nonsense about Prayer (Chicago: Moody Press, 1974), 25-29.

he must wait on God. By doing this, the missionary demonstrates to the Father that he seeks God alone and His good pleasure, and not the selfish delights of his own satisfaction.[105] He must bring his thoughts into conformity with the mind of Christ. The missionary cannot automatically assume that he is doing God's will simply because he is a missionary. He must search his own motives and God's will anew each day.

The prayer life of the missionary can easily become self-centered. Prayer energy can be spent totally on one's work rather than getting to know God. "When Jesus looked out on the mission field, the first thing he instructed his disciples to do was to pray (Matthew 9:38). Workers are necessary, their work is necessary, but before anything else comes prayer."[106] It is imperative that all missionaries listen to God's will and submit themselves in obedience to it. Do missionaries call God to witness to their activities as the Apostle Paul did in front of the Philippians?

The more intimately the missionary knows God, the more clearly he will be able to see God's purposes in the circumstances that come into current events. The missionary must align his will with God's will, for this is when prayers really become effective. God wants the missionary to pray for His divine purpose, and therefore prayer must seek God first before it seeks petitions from God. All true prayer stems from a pure heart.

---

[105]Madame Guyon, <u>Experience God through Prayer</u> (Chicago: Moody Press, 1974), 25-29.

[106]Thomas Hale, <u>On Being a Missionary</u> (Springdale, PA: Whitaker House, 1984), 25-26.

David the psalmist intimates that every prayer should begin by setting the Lord before the mind's eye (Psalm 16:8). Whoever or whatever is absent from any prayer, the Lord should always be present. The missionary should never kneel without shutting his eyes to earthly things and setting his eyes upon God Himself.[107]

God seems removed when the heart is not pure. Missionaries who are self-absorbed do not focus on God. When attention is placed on one's own problems and plans, the heart grows indifferent to the spiritual and physical needs around him. Christians who have a critical and grumbling spirit will find their prayers hindered. In order for prayer to be effective, the entire will must be submitted to God. The missionary should long for the will of God as Paul did. When intimacy with God is destroyed, prayers are blocked.[108]

The Purpose of Prayer

Prayer that is offered from a pure heart to God always serves a definite purpose. "Prayer with the Father will bring you and your colleagues into a relationship of fellowship and listening for the Master's guidance."[109] In other words, prayer that is offered from a pure heart and from within a proper relationship with Christ will also

---

[107]Alexander Whyte, Lord, Teach Us to Pray (Grand Rapids: Baker Book House, 1976), 99-102.

[108]Hale, 333-34.

[109]Sherwood Lingenfelter, Agents of Transformation (Grand Rapids: Baker Book House, 1996), 260.

form the basis for the loving compassion needed to identify with the people of one's calling.[110]

A cursory glance at the book of Philippians reveals that the Apostle Paul frequently prayed for the well-being of his converts. "Paul's manifold requests were primarily related to the growth in Christian maturity of the readers."[111] The apostle frequently used terms that refer to his readers' full maturity in Christ, terms such as "fullness," "abundance," and "riches."

Thus, Philippians 1:9-11 serves as an outlet for Paul's feelings, as they are expressed in verses seven and eight. Paul interceded for the Philippians in order that their love might grow. He desired that this love would grow in knowledge and tact in order that the Philippians might be able to distinguish the really important issues of life. The ultimate goal of Paul's intercession was that the Philippian believers may be "filled with the fruits of righteousness" (1:11). It was Paul's desire that the Philippian church be filled with godly deeds and actions.[112]

Paul, then, was not praying for a release from jail as might be expected. Whether he was acquitted or not, his

---

[110]Harold R. Carpenter, "An Introduction to Assemblies of God Missions for Use at Central Bible College" (D.Miss. diss., Trinity Evangelical Divinity School, 1988), 162.

[111]Peter T. O'Brien, "The Fellowship Theme in Philippians," Reformed Theological Review 37, no. 1 (1978), 15.

[112]O'Brien, 15.

71

prayer was that the Philippians be girded and strengthened. As is true in so many other instances, Paul was
praying for spiritual benefits rather than physical well-
being.[113] These spiritual benefits include spiritual vision,
spiritual vitality, and spiritual victory

Spiritual Vision

Paul prayed that the Philippian love for fellow believers would develop in the areas of knowledge and judgment. The first word, "knowledge," generally conveys the
idea of a mental grasp of truth. When a Christian has a
better knowledge of God and His ways, greater harmony
is promoted within the fellowship. The Philippians, then,
would have a clearer understanding of their mutual relationship with each other if they had a greater spiritual vision of God.[114]

The second word, translated "judgment," refers to per-
ception, discrimination, or even tact. "It is the employment of the faculty which makes a person able to make a
moral decision."[115] Paul, then, wanted the Philippians to
have a greater spiritual vision of God that would result in
a greater spiritual vision of what was and what was not
acceptable Christian behavior. This was one of the purposes of his prayer.

---

[113]William B. Park, "The Strategy for Local Church
Missions" (D.Min. diss., Faith Theological Seminary,
1983), 176.

[114]Martin, 66.

[115]Martin, 66.

In the Old Testament, Hezekiah sought an answer from God with regard to Sennacherib's siege of Jerusalem. The Bible reports that Sennacherib prayed to the Lord, and the Lord answered him through the prophet Isaiah. Hezekiah was informed that Sennacherib definitely would not enter the city. A plague struck the Assyrian camp that night, and Sennacherib withdrew and was slain shortly after returning to his capital. Through the vehicle of prayer, the king of Judah had both knowledge of God's plan, and knowledge of how he should behave in light of God's plan.[116]

The application to missions could not be more poignant. Frequently, the missionary does not know the will of God or how to behave in light of the will of God. Nothing gives more spiritual vision to these issues than prayer. Paul knew that he was to be a missionary, but the knowledge of where that call was to be fulfilled was only gained through prayer. It was only as Paul sought the mind of the Holy Spirit that he received the vision to go into Macedonia (Acts 16:6-10). Indeed, Paul could have remained as a teacher in Antioch had there not been prayer for knowledge and judgment (Acts 13:1-4). It was in the midst of a fast that the Holy Spirit gave a vision for the unreached people groups of the world.[117]

This is why it is so important for missionaries to start their planning sessions with prayer. When field leaders begin their planning sessions this way, it helps to create

---

[116]Lingenfelter, 176.

[117]Leo M. Thornton, "A Study of the Missionary Call as Found in Acts of the Apostles and in Modern Missionary Biography" (B.D. diss., Western Evangelical Seminary, 1952), 36.

the right atmosphere for discerning the mind of the Lord. When missionaries begin by asking God to lead them, they very seldom have to apologize for their activities.[118] If the missionary wants to lead his converts securely into the future, he must pray for knowledge and judgment, that is, spiritual vision.

Spiritual Vitality

In addition to spiritual vision, the missionary must pray for spiritual vitality. If the Philippian believers acquired the virtues of knowledge and judgment, they would be able to "approve things that are excellent" and "be sincere and without offense" (1:10).

The word *approve* means "to put to the test," and then as a result of the examination, "to accept as tested, to approve." The term was often used to denote the testing of coins. The coins that were approved were accepted as genuine currency. The prayer of the Apostle Paul was that the Philippian believers would be able to ascertain what really mattered. He desired that his friends would have the ability to discern and then practice in their Christian living the important issues of life.[119]

The reader, however, is not left in the dark as to what the important issues of life are. The Christian is called to live sincerely and without offense. The word *sincere* is possibly derived from the word for sunlight. If so, this

---

[118]Donald C. Palmer, "Development of a Manual on Conflict Management for Training GMU Missionaries" (D. Min. diss., Trinity Evangelical Divinity School, 1990), 62.

[119]Martin, 67.

continues the thought of testing. The believer is to live as if we were being tested by the exacting standards of clear sunlight and shown to be unmixed, pure, and genuine. In other words, the Christian is to possess a transparency that is free from all impurity. As the second phrase explains, the Christian is to be "without offense," that is, blameless.[120]

Not only is the missionary to pray for a vision of God's will, he is to pray for a vitality to practice that will. The purpose of knowing the will of God is to practice it. "There is nothing more powerful than prayer to cause miraculous events in missions."[121]

This is why many mission organizations are concerned about the prayer life of the missionary candidate. God's resources that enable the missionary to do God's work are released through prayer. While it is true that prayer is necessary for all Christians, the lack of prayer will be felt more acutely on the mission field where vitality is so necessary.[122] In a mysterious way, the activity of the Holy Spirit is released through prayer. "Prayer itself has no power, but it acts as an ignition switch by which we can tap the power of the Spirit."[123]

---

[120]Martin, 68.

[121]Kyung Taeg Lim, "A Comparative Analysis of Programming and Budgeting for Mission Fund Development in Local Churches of Kwangju, Kyunggi Province, Korea" (D.Miss. diss., Western Seminary, 1999), 44.

[122]Hale, 43.

[123]Hale, 335.

Every missionary will face his "Peniel" experience (Genesis 23:26). There are times when he must, like Jacob, grasp by faith and wrestle with the Lord all night. The missionary must seek the promised blessing and not "let God go" until this is received. This is how the missionary becomes a true man of God and is recognized as a prince. Though physical disabilities may come from such wrestling matches, these times with God are not to be viewed as defeats, but victories. The missionary cannot be passive or timid in his prayer life if he wishes to survive as one who has power with God. The blessing comes through a fight to the finish. In prayer the missionary must face God without fear, grasp God in faith, and expect the reality of God's blessings. Are our current missionary candidates prepared to toil all night with God in prayer? Are they prepared to not let God go until they are blessed? Unless they are, they will never know the vitality of missionary life.[124]

Frankly, many missionaries do not believe in prayer. They do not pray through. Many do not seem to realize that in order to experience vitality, there must be constant heart-searching in long hours of prayer coupled with fasting, confession, and restitution. When God's people really pray through, they can have revival and receive God's protection, provision, and anointing.[125]

Scripture paints prayer as vitally important in the life of the missionary. Apart from Jesus, the missionary can

---

[124]Joseph L. Cannon, For Missionaries Only (Grand Rapids: Baker Book House, 1975), 82-84.

[125]John R. Rice, Prayer — Asking and Receiving (Murfreesboro, TN: Sword of the Lord Publishers, 1942), 213.

do nothing (John 15:5). Human strategies, plans, and efforts will be totally ineffective unless there is prayer to energize them. Paul taught and modeled prayer as the means to advance the Gospel. He prayed for the salvation of the Jews. He asked others to pray for the Gospel to spread and for his witness to be bold. He prayed that his converts would do good works and have wise discernment. He prayed for personal strength and endurance. He received mercy and grace through prayer. Paul recognized that the prayers of a righteous man are effective and powerful (James 5:16). The apostle Paul recognized that prayer was essential for spiritual vitality. There is no way to have discernment and purity without it.[126]

Spiritual Victory

A final aspiration of Paul in this prayer for his readers is that their lives might be "filled with the fruits of righteousness" (1:11). The "fruits of righteousness" are the evidences of a right relationship with God in the display of ethical characteristics, which are described in Galatians 5:22. In other words, it is conduct that is pleasing to God.[127]

When Christ returns, each person's character will be evaluated. Has that person trusted in God's divinely provided righteousness? Does his life evidence the fruit of such faith? It should be the goal of every Christian, especially every missionary, to live a life that brings glory to

---

[126]Robert B. Stanbery, "The Role of the Senior Pastor in Influencing His Congregation Towards Word Evangelization" (Th.M. diss., Dallas Theological Seminary, 2000), 14-16.

[127]Martin, 68-69.

God. The life of the missionary should be praiseworthy. This was the prayer request of Paul. He wanted his life and the lives of those he had won to the Lord to be victorious.[128]

It is true that prayer is no magic formula. Some missionaries have left the field or have fallen ill in spite of the fact that they had great prayer support. Nevertheless, prayer is essential to fruitfulness and power. Transmitters can beam radio waves into closed countries. Missionaries can witness to unbelievers. It is prayer, however, that opens hearts to receive the message. "Prayer is essential to the success of everything we do. Let our prayers be large; our God is not small."[129] There can be no victory without prayer.

The early church depended on prayer in the missionary enterprise. They prayed that they would witness boldly (Acts 4:29-30). Missionaries were sent into the world as a result of their fasting and prayer (Acts 13:2-3). Prayer was also used to ascertain God's will in the appointment of spiritual leadership for the churches planted by missionaries (Acts 14:23). No stage of the missionary's work is victorious without prayer.

Stanbery gives two significant reasons why prayer is the key to victory. First, it is the communication link between the missionary and the Lord. It is through prayer that the missionary receives specific instructions and strategy in his effort to evangelize the lost. Second, prayer is the key weapon of spiritual warfare for the missionary. It brings more laborers (Matthew 9:38), helps defeat the

---

[128]Martin, 69.

[129]Hale, 334.

devil (Matthew 6:13), results in more fruit (John 15:16), and unleashes the power of the Word (Ephesians 6:18-20). It stabilizes the world so that men might hear the Gospel without being distracted by worldly interruptions.[130]

Jesus told His disciples that they were being sent to bear fruit (John 15:16). As they went, if they prayed in His name, the Father would grant their requests to aid in their bearing of fruit. Spiritual fruitfulness is directly linked to prayer. Similarly, Paul urges that prayers be made on behalf of all men because God wants all men to be saved and to come to a knowledge of the truth (I Timothy 2:1-4). Men cannot be saved without prayer.[131] It is the key to the missionary's victory. "Spiritual teams work through spiritual means. If the spiritual means aren't there, the team will do no spiritual work."[132]

Prayer and the Prospective Missionary

Jesus Christ is the perfect and eternal high priest, and there is no longer a human, earthly institution of priests as there was in the Old Testament. Nevertheless, all believers are priests (I Peter 2:5). Jesus Christ "has made us kings and priests unto God" (Revelation 1:6). In that sense, the entire body of believers is a priesthood. Christians do not have to go through a human mediator to reach God. They are able to have direct communication and fellowship with God through prayer. In addition, each believer can engage in a priestly ministry of bringing others

---

[130]Stanbery, 16.

[131]Stanbery, 17.

[132]Hale, 220.

into the presence of God. This is particularly true of the missionary.

Paul, the missionary, did not inherit a priestly office by birth, but he was a priest in the sense that all Christians are priests. During his missionary travels, Paul would start preaching and teaching in a city or town. As Paul preached, he would be used of God to bring some people to Christ. His special calling was to be a "minister of Jesus Christ to the Gentiles" (Romans 15:16).

The word translated "minister" was frequently used by the Greeks to refer to public officials. In the New Testament, however, the word is used most often to describe those who serve God in some form of public worship.[133] Figuratively, Paul ministered the Gospel of God as a priest. He did so in order that he might present an offering of Gentiles unto the Lord. In faithful fulfillment of his missionary calling, Paul's supreme offering to God was a multitude of Gentiles who by virtue of the Holy Spirit's power had been sanctified and thus made acceptable for fellowship with the Father. Like Paul, every missionary who is instrumental in winning a soul to Jesus Christ presents that convert, whether Jew or Gentile, as a priestly offering to the Lord.[134]

The priestly function of the missionary does not stop there, however. A priest is a man who does not live for himself. He lives with God and for God. His work is to care for God's house, God's honor, and God's worship.

---

[133]Luke 1:23; Philippians 2:17; Hebrews 1:7, 14; 8:1-2,6.

[134]John F. MacArthur, Jr., <u>Romans 9-16</u> (Chicago: Moody Press, 1994), 331-32.

The priest is responsible to make known to men God's love and God's will. The priest, therefore, also lives with men and for men. He is to find out the sin of his people and bring it before God in prayer.[135] In short, the priest is to be an intercessor.

The missionary who fails to stand before God on behalf of the people to whom he ministers has failed in his priestly role. Each day the missionary should stand before God and pray that those who have been committed to his care will experience spiritual vision, vitality, and victory. It is only as the missionary places the Lord in view through prayer that he shall never be moved. (Psalm 16:8).

---

[135]Andrew Murray, With Christ in the School of Prayer (Grand Rapids: Zondervan Publishing House, 1983), 153.

Chapter 5
Contentment

When Jesus commissioned His disciples to go and preach the Gospel, His financial requirements were less stringent than those of many mission boards today. His commissioning mandate is fascinatingly simple: "Take nothing for your journey, neither staves, nor scrip, neither bread, neither money" (Luke 9:3). The modern missionary, however, often does not share Luke's desire for simplicity. Relative to American standards, the missionary may live modestly, but in relation to the people he seeks to evangelize, the missionary's financial status can be described with no other word than "luxurious."[136]

Many American missionaries consider simply going to the field a sacrifice. Living on the level of the nationals is considered too much to ask, even if deciding to do so would greatly improve their inculturation and opportunities for evangelism. This reluctance suggests that the missionary must develop "a reasonable contentment with a more modest living standard."[137]

On many mission fields the missionaries are the only ones with good and decent homes, clean water, electricity, telephone service, and automobiles. Often missionaries employ nationals as servants to assist with their cooking and gardening. Missionaries are frequently viewed as the privileged members of society, and unfortunately, many nationals assume that affluence and wealth are part of the Christian package. Disillusionment sets in, however,

---

[136]Jonathan J. Bonk, <u>Missions and Money</u> (Maryknoll, NY: Orbis Books, 1991), xi.

[137]Bonk, xiii.

when new converts do not see any improvement in their material and social status because they have become Christians.[138]

When one examines the example of the Savior, however, he is presented with a vastly different model. The life of Christ was a life of self-denial. This self-denial is the very heart of the Gospel. It is unfortunate that the lives of many missionaries contradict the message they are seeking to articulate. The Gospel is frequently hindered by "insensitive affluence" that makes social relationships difficult and embarrassing. The economic gap that exists between missionaries and nationals makes friendship virtually impossible.[139]

Missionary affluence almost seems to be a contradiction in terms. Compared to most North American Christians, the missionary has indeed left houses and relatives for the sake of Jesus (Matthew 19:27-30). To the contemporary American, the missionary is a living example of sacrifice. These same missionaries, however, are viewed as rich in the country where they minister. Herein lies the problem. More than one hundred years ago, James Gilmour put the blame for ineffective missionary effort on an expensive European lifestyle, and nothing has been done in the past century to answer this critique. Mission agencies have been unwilling or unable to pay the price.[140]

Obviously, change is difficult. Americans from the time of infancy are taught consumerism. The goal of

---

[138]Bonk, xiv.

[139]Bonk, xv.

[140]Bonk, xvii, 10, 13.

human life is bigger and better things. In short, most Americans do believe that "life consists in the abundance of things that a man possesses." It is not surprising, therefore, to find American missionaries who are eager to put the latest gadgets into missionary service. Suppliers now exist for the purpose of ensuring that missionaries do not become out-of-date in their technology. Indeed, most American supporting churches see nothing wrong with this; they actually encourage it. Biblical teachings on greed and covetousness are virtually ignored, and such activity is considered necessary. This activity, however, has caused some nationals to think that American missionaries have arrived with the sole intention of taking a vacation in a foreign country.[141]

Unfortunately there are not many significant works that have attempted to deal with this problem. Even those who are experts in the field are forced to admit that "there are no easy answers to the perplexing and sometimes ministry-destroying effects of missionary affluence."[142] A look to the book of Philippians (1:12-26), however, reveals some helpful guidelines.

The Gospel over Comfort

In this passage of Scripture the Apostle Paul is greatly encouraged because Christ is being proclaimed. His confinement in prison is not curtailing the ministry of the Gospel, but has led to an extension of the Gospel. Therefore, Paul is content to be in jail. Even "the rivalry and misdirected zeal" of other believers cannot obscure the fact that the message of Christ is being preached.

---

[141]Bonk, 27-29, 46.

[142]Bonk, xviii.

Certainly imprisonment would cause many missionaries frustration and despair, but in Paul's case, it only increased his joy. Paul was content because the higher interests of the Gospel were being served.[143]

The Philippians naturally wanted to know how prison life was affecting Paul. The information given in these verses (1:12-18) is Paul's "disclosure formula," his reply relating his present circumstances. What had happened to Paul was for "the furtherance of the gospel" (1:12). The Gospel had advanced in spite of obstructions and dangers that sought to impede its path. The chief obstacle, of course, was Paul's confinement in prison. Although Paul's activity had been restricted through this incarceration, his confinement had actually resulted in a powerful witness for Christ. The Gospel was triumphing in a pagan world.[144]

Paul had been imprisoned because of his adherence to Christ, but the confinement was not just for Christ, it was literally "in Christ" (1:13). In other words, Paul was a prisoner in union with his Lord. He bore his sufferings "in Christ," and this "gave point and power to his witness."[145] The praetorian guards came in contact with Paul in the course of their duties, and consequently other pagans and Christians came to hear of Paul's arrest and the reason for it (1:13).

---

[143]Ralph P. Martin, The Epistle of Paul to the Philippians (Grand Rapids: Eerdmans Publishing Company, 1987), 69.

[144]Martin, 70.

[145]Martin, 70.

The Christians who received the news were so encouraged by Paul's fortitude that they began to give a bolder testimony to the Word of God than they previously had done (1:14). As Paul received word of their fearlessness, he became all the more contented in his confinement. The Gospel's advance meant more to him than personal comfort.[146]

Many Christians became involved in evangelistic efforts even though they were not all governed by the same motives. Some preached the word out of "envy and strife" while others proclaimed it out of "good will" (1:15). The consequence was that many were speaking the Word with new zeal even though some were ill-intentioned.

It is assumed, then, that these witnesses were not pagans using the name of Christ in blasphemy. It also follows that they were not heretics who were taking advantage of Paul's incarceration to propagate false teaching. They appear to have been Christians who had no personal affinity for the Apostle Paul. Thus they tried to make his imprisonment "as galling and irksome as possible."[147]

Their "envy and strife" were directed against Paul personally. Their preaching of Christ was initiated by "contention." They wanted to add "affliction" to Paul's bonds (1:16). The Greek term θλιψιν refers to a friction and serves as a vivid reminder of the painful rubbing of iron chains on the apostle's hands and legs. These

---

[146]Martin, 71.

[147]Martin, 73.

"preachers" wanted to irritate Paul as he lay helpless in prison and unable to defend himself.[148]

Recent commentators have interpreted the cryptic reference to Christians who preach Christ yet emphasize a message Paul could not accept as men who could not accept the apostle because he was a suffering missionary. Envy and animosity motivated these men, because in their view, Paul had discredited the Christian message by his imprisonment. They, therefore, had developed a rival strategy that emphasized power and glory rather than pain and suffering.[149]

Other preachers, however, recognized that Paul was put in jail "for the defense of the gospel" (1:17). His friends knew that his imprisonment was because of his devotion to Christ and His cause. With this understanding in mind, they preached Christ with "good will" (1:15) and "love" (1:16).

Through all of this, Paul recognized that he had been put in jail for a purpose. He used the term κειμαι, a military term. He was enduring hardness as a good soldier of Jesus Christ (2 Timothy 2:3-4), and he was just as much "on duty" as "the guards posted to watch over him [were] on duty in the service of Rome."[150]

Thus, all evil designs were in vain as far as their personal effect upon the apostle was concerned. Christ was being proclaimed, and if that was the case, Paul was

---

[148]Martin, 73.

[149]Martin, 75.

[150]Martin, 75.

content. What did the motives of men matter? Even though human beings may have had a conflict of loyalties and there was division within the Christian community, Paul was content because of one all-important fact. "Whether in pretense, or in truth, Christ [was] preached" (1:18).

Paul's ability to place the Gospel over personal comfort provided a great enhancement to his evangelistic efforts. The essence of evangelism is communication, and communication takes place both in verbal and nonverbal ways. It is imperative, therefore, that the missionary does not destroy the message of his lips by the style of his life. The expensive lifestyles of many missionaries frequently ensure that their good news is not heard.[151]

When a missionary preaches the Gospel of salvation with his lips, and the gospel of affluence with his life, his presence does not create a hunger or thirst for righteousness. Rather, his presence stimulates within his potential converts a desire for the affluence of Western culture.[152]

Whatever gains a missionary may achieve with affluence must be evaluated against the losses that he will suffer in his communication of the Gospel. Clinging to material goods makes identification with the poor impossible. It creates a dichotomy between missionary teaching and missionary living. It causes the good news of God to be corrupted by the "death-producing gospel of mammon."[153]

---

[151]Bonk, 60.

[152]Bonk, 67.

[153]Bonk, 68.

Every decision made by a missionary should be governed by the impact that this decision will have on the Gospel. Unfortunately, many missionaries choose not to be governed by this principle. Those who are, however, produce a witness that impacts unbelievers both in immediate as well as long-term ways, which in turn creates a greater acceptance of the Gospel. Affluence and poverty are not the central problems per se. The question is how they impact the acceptance of the Gospel.[154]

When a missionary becomes consumed with materialism, he becomes program-oriented. Rather than identifying with the people he has been called to reach, he relies on charts and graphs. Personal relationships are replaced with mobility and speed. The missionary becomes preoccupied with running and maintaining technological aids of comfort and efficiency, and has little time left for missionary work.[155] To quote Francis, "Jesus' way of communicating the love of God by participating in human aspirations, struggles and hopes and enabling and empowering the weak, the oppressed and the marginalized to enjoy in full their basic rights is the pattern set before Christian communicators."[156] It is imperative for every missionary to assume the Pauline model in Philippians and place the advance of the Gospel over personal comfort.

---

[154]Hendrik De Vries, "A Missionary's Economic Decision-Making in the Context of Disparity" (Th.M. diss., Calvin Theological Seminary, 1989), 70, 78.

[155]Bonk, 71.

[156]T. Dayanandan Francis, "Gospel and Communication," Arasaradi Journal of Theological Reflection 5, no.1 (1992), 138.

Paul was also content because he counted on two kinds of aid: human prayers and the divine help of the Holy Spirit (1:19). The same Spirit that dwelled so richly in Christ Jesus resided in the apostle as well. This Holy Spirit was a welcome "supply" to the imprisoned missionary. The word "supply" translates the Greek word επιχορηγιας, which refers to an assistance that undergirds and strengthens an object. The strength of the Spirit allowed the Apostle Paul to look at the things that had happened, that is, his imprisonment, and recognize that there was a divine purpose behind it. The strength of the Spirit also allowed the apostle to look to the future and see a certain salvation. This "salvation" (1:19) cannot be a reference to his release from imprisonment in view of the next verse where he envisions the possibility of death. The term must be a reference to Paul's personal final salvation (Romans 13:11).[157] Because Paul had been reinforced by the prayers of believers, and consequently by the supply of the Spirit, he was not afraid to die.

On the contrary, Paul possessed an "earnest expectation" and "hope" that caused him to face the future with "boldness" (1:20). The apostle used a picturesque Greek term to express his earnest expectation. The word αποκαραδοκιαν denotes "a keen anticipation of the future, the craning of the neck to catch a glimpse of what lies ahead, the concentrated intense hope that ignores other interests and strains forward as with an outstretched head."[158]

---

[157]Martin, 76-77.

[158]Martin, 78.

If Paul were released, Christ would be magnified by a continuance of his missionary activity. If Paul died as a martyr, Christ would still have been glorified by his faithful testimony unto death. The apostle boldly stated, "Christ shall be magnified in my body, whether it be by life, or by death." (1:20). "The alternatives" between life and death, "so tremendous to us, [were] seen by the apostle as leading to the same end: the glory of the Lord."[159]

Paul appeared to be hesitant to reveal his preference. He did not know which one to choose (1:22). If he continued to live in this fleshly existence, a continued life of ministry would follow. His missionary labor, here described as "the fruit of my labor," would expand. The choice is between a continuation of work and a sealing of his testimony with martyrdom. When confronted with these two alternatives, Paul confessed that he could not decide which one was better.[160] The pressure of opposite forces put Paul in a difficult situation. He was "hemmed in on both sides and prevented by the equal strength of opposing forces from inclining one way or the other."[161] He was torn between the two options (1:23).

For the apostle Paul, "to live is Christ, and to die is gain" (1:21). The "gain" here refers "not only to the apostle's own receiving of his heavenly reward in the presence of his Master, but the promotion of the gospel in the witness that his fearless martyrdom for Christ will

---

[159]Martin, 78.

[160]Martin, 80.

[161]Martin, 81.

produce."[162] Death would have been gain because it would have advanced the proclamation of the Gospel. In both life and death Paul was dedicated to the service of the Lord.

If, however, the apostle were left to his own inclination, the option would be clear. He would choose "to depart and to be with Christ" (1:23). Though the word "desire" is normally used in the New Testament in a bad sense, this is a noticeable exception. Paul possessed this desire because he was confident that death provided entrance into the presence of Christ. Thus, Paul had a desire "to depart." The term is a military term for striking camp or a nautical expression used to describe the release of a boat from its moorings. Although Paul already lived in intimate union with his Lord, he desired an even greater intimacy. This desire would be fulfilled when Paul reached heaven. The privilege to "be with Christ" was "far better" (1:23).

For the Christian there is no "unconscious state" or "purgatorial discipline" after death. Paul expected death to usher him into the very presence of Christ. "Many things about the future beyond the grave are veiled from us; but what has been revealed is all we need to know.[163] When the Christian dies, he is "absent from the body" and "present with the Lord" (2 Corinthians 5:8). Because Paul had a proper understanding of death as "gain," he was able to rise above materialism and live a contented life.

Unfortunately, many missionaries have not maintained this perspective. In Western culture the "seven deadly

---

[162]Martin, 79.

[163]Martin, 82-83.

92

sins" are often viewed as positive virtues. This inversion of Biblical values should be of vital concern to those who are preparing to go to the mission field. Paul forcefully condemned Western consumerism with its attendant problems, not only by his example, but also by his writings. A church leader should not be a lover of money (I Timothy 3:3). According to Paul, it is the lost who are characterized by a continual craving for more (Ephesians 4:19). These are sobering words to those who "have come to expect as their due steady improvement in an already high standard of living."[164]

When a missionary seeks a secure, independent, comfortable lifestyle, he loses his genuine dependence upon God. He has not counted being with Christ as "far better." In the Old Testament, security and wealth frequently gave rise to foolish and fatal independence. God's admonition to His people was to beware when they had eaten and become satisfied, lest they forget the Lord (Deuteronomy 6:11-12). Missionaries need to heed this admonition. All too frequently, trust in God is replaced by trust in money, and prayer letters become thinly veiled appeals for financial support rather than requests for "prayer and the supply of the Spirit" (1:19). Affluence makes God necessary only in an academic or theological sense.[165]

A strong case can be made that many missionaries show no great willingness to lose all things for the sake of Jesus Christ (Philippians 3:7-8). Indeed, the things that Paul counted as loss, many missionaries count as absolutely essential for the continuation of mission work. This

---

[164]Bonk, 80.

[165]Bonk, 80-81.

complete reversal of values has placed the missionary in direct opposition to the examples of Paul and Christ.

When Christ was tempted to prove His relation to God by demonstrations of power and strength, He utterly rejected the temptation (Matthew 4:1-11). His mission work would unfold "in poverty, weakness, and obscurity."[166] The earthly career of Christ began and ended with renunciation. As Jonathan Bonk[167] rightly observes, "This does not leave much room for the power-generating, status-inflating, career-building, self-protecting affluence to which emissaries of the Western churches have become accustomed."[168]

Some have suggested that American missionaries should not try to identify with a culture they are attempting to evangelize if, in the eyes of that culture, they have a right to a higher status. That misunderstanding and suspicion will take place no one can deny. This, however, is not a sufficient reason to continue to enjoy the benefits of materialism. Jesus suffered lifelong misunderstanding and suspicion because he "made himself of no reputation and took upon himself the form of a servant" (Philippians 2:7). This eventually resulted in death.

---

[166]Bonk, 116.

[167]The fact that Jonathan Bonk is published by the Catholic Foreign Mission Society of America (Maryknoll) should not disguise the fact that he is a Canadian Mennonite. By the publisher's own admission, Bonk writes predominantly in reference to Protestant missions, especially those in North America.

[169]Bonk, 117.

Much that is distinctive in the presentation of the Gospel does run counter to societal norms. Those who are bold enough to surrender their lives in selfless service often will be regarded as a threat. The wisdom of God appears to be foolishness to men (I Corinthians 2:14).

The time has come for American missionaries to return to this "foolishness." "No matter how enlightened the technique, how massive the budget, how sophisticated the technology, or how numerous the well-qualified personnel, nothing but God's strategy revealed in the Incarnation will prevail."[169] No matter how strange or inappropriate this strategy may appear to the target culture, it is the only method that will work in spiritual battle.

The Incarnation has a profound impact upon the lifestyle of the missionary when he implements the qualities of Christ as Christ incarnated God among the people of His day. Christ emptied Himself of His privileged status and took upon Himself the limitations of humanity. The obvious application is that all missionaries should adopt this model.[170]

Unfortunately, many mission organizations today go to great lengths to prove their desire to meet the needs and wants of their missionaries. Comprehensive support packages ensure that missionaries will never learn "how to be abased" (Philippians 4:12). The missionary and his family consequently never learn how to be content regardless of their state (Philippians 4:11). New Testament teaching on

---

[169]Bonk, 117.

[170]DeVries, 14.

self-denial is thrown away for a comfortable life abroad.[171]

The Apostle Paul, however, from the moment he was called into missionary service, learned that this was a life of suffering and denial (Acts 9:16). To be a missionary meant to become the "scum of the earth" (I Corinthians 4:8-13). "Like his Savior's before him, Paul's life did not have a happy ending, a 'missionary statesman' surrounded by devoted supporters and fellow veterans in a Christian retirement village somewhere in the Mediterranean."[172] He spent his last days isolated in a Roman jail, and then his life was finally taken by a powerful state. By human standards, he was a failure. Like the Lord, however, Paul proved that "to die is gain" (1:21).

Others Over Self

Although Paul wanted to be with Christ in heaven, he knew his personal desire must be subordinated to his ministerial responsibility to the Philippians. The down-to-earth needs of his fellow believers were of greater importance than his own feelings. It was "more needful" (1:24) for the Philippian Christians that he remain.[173]

Because this was the "needful" thing, Paul was confident it would become reality. He boldly stated, "I know that I shall abide and continue with you all" (1:25). He foresaw a return to Philippi and a resumption of ministry in their midst. Paul possessed this "confidence" because

---

[171]Bonk, 119.

[172]Bonk, 121.

[173]Martin, 82.

he knew it was the will of God for their Christian lives to advance, for their joy to deepen, and their faith to be enlarged. When their prayers were answered and the Apostle Paul came to them again (1:26), it would promote their joy and confirm their faith (1:25). The Philippians would have good reason to praise the Lord because of Paul's release, and Paul made it clear that his triumphant return would be the occasion for this exultation (1:26). Thus, Paul, using a very strong word, called upon the Philippians to rejoice.[174]

Here the third reason for Paul's remarkable contentment is revealed. In addition to placing the Gospel over comfort and death over life, the apostle was able to place others over self. "Paul [manifested] an impressive belief in, and concern for, development of the Christian faith among his readers."[175] Paul was confident that God, who began a good work, would finish it in the lives of His people (Philippians 1:6). Thus, Paul was confident that he would be used to help the Philippians progress and joy in their faith (1:25). With remarkable frequency, Paul used the word "rejoice" to designate the spirit of the believing community, and he constantly urged a spirit of thankfulness for the beliefs of salvation.[176]

Unfortunately, this desire for spiritual development in the lives of the nationals is not seen in many modern missionaries. Sometimes missionaries are perceived as nothing more than vacationers in a foreign country. Sites for

---

[174]Martin, 83-84.

[175]Patrick Rogers, "Hopeful in Spite of Chains," Biblical Theology Bulletin 12, no. 3 (1982), 78.

[176]Rogers, 79.

"ministry bases" are chosen because of their comfortable, sunny climates. Often missionaries proceed to live in a society limited to themselves. They close themselves up in little compound to be alone. Contact is not sought with others, and missionaries are not open to friendships.[177]

Much of this is attributable to the social gulf that exists between the missionary and the national. In friendships, people naturally gravitate to those who are socially and economically equal. Wealthy families do not normally share deep fraternal relationships with families whose incomes are much lower than their own.[178]

In addition, the affluence of many missionaries causes them to think of themselves as teachers rather than servants of the poor. It is difficult to behave like a servant when one is rich and powerful.[179]

Because missionaries often enjoy considerable material and social advantages, the motives of the missionary may be suspect. Many missionaries have discovered that their presence, rather than causing a hunger and thirst for righteousness, caused a hunger and thirst for material things. Frequently the nationals are indifferent to the missionary's words because of their rapt preoccupation with the missionary's things. The national, if he does come close to the missionary, does so for personal profit rather than spiritual salvation. The missionary, in turn, denounces the culture in which he "ministers" as covetousness, when in

---

[177]Bonk, 46-47.

[178]Bonk, 48-49.

[179]Bonk, 52.

fact it was his lifestyle that created the desire for more. The missionary has no one to blame but himself for the confusion.[180] The missionary has taught the national that the human soul is not worth as much as the things of this world.

Sacrifice and the Missionary Candidate

Many important Biblical characters received their notoriety because of what they were willing to sacrifice. Jeremiah sacrificed friendship and the status of the priesthood to preach the truth of God. Stephen gave his life in martyrdom rather than compromise the message of the Gospel. The ability to sacrifice has a direct bearing upon the missionary task. The Apostle Paul's career cannot be analyzed properly without an evaluation of his suffering. The apostle had a firm belief that transcultural communication is most effective through the strength of weakness.[181]

If, then, the American missionary wants to be a significant force in this world, he must seriously grapple with the issue of affluence. Those who continue to demonstrate the gospel of abundance will generate envy and hostility rather than legitimate conversions. "Medium and message are both significantly affected by the relationship of the missionary to the convert or would-be convert."[182] The message of the cross is more than just a series of theologically correct propositions; the message must be incarnated in the life of the evangelist. A missionary must not simply

---

[180]Bonk, 53-54.

[181]DeVries, 66.

[182]Bonk, 58.

announce the way; he must show it.[183] This demands that the missionary be a content pilgrim, embracing the Gospel over comfort, death over life, and others over self.

It is obviously not God's will that all missionaries remain in one place, or even one country. It is obvious, however, that God asks the missionary to be content in his area of placement. Those who have been called to be fishers of men should not return to their secular professions simply because they have suffered disappointment. Many current missionaries have "boats" and "nets" available for a quick move from the ministry to secular pursuits (John 21:3). The Lord, however, states that the fisher of men should love Christ more than these things (John 21:15). Christ is looking for men who will be content to remain in missionary service.[184] Such men have already chosen the Gospel over comfort, death over life, and others over self.

---

[183]Bonk, 57-58.

[184]Joseph L. Cannon, For Missionaries Only (Grand Rapids: Baker Book House, 1975), 88-90.

Chapter 6
Pulpit Ministry

In the ministry of Jesus, preaching was given a place of prominence. Though there were many methods He could have used, Jesus chose to come into the world preaching. In the synagogue at Nazareth He described Himself as having been divinely ordained to preach (Luke 4:18). This same methodology was passed on to the apostles. Preaching was in the announced purpose for them; they were told to go into the entire world and preach the Gospel to every creature (Mark 16:15). In the book of Acts and in the Epistles of the New Testament, the record and influence of their preaching are found.[185]

Preaching, therefore, is a necessity to Christian ministry, for preaching is inextricably linked to the life of the church. The church was brought into existence through preaching, and preaching is the only thing that can keep life in the church. "Christian history has demonstrated that the strength of the church is directly related to the strength of the pulpit."[186] When the pulpit of the church has been weak, the church itself has been weak. When, however, the pulpit of the church has been strong, the church itself has been strong. The work of missions is directly tied to effective preaching.

It is not surprising, therefore, to discover that the Apostle Paul was a gifted preacher. He had an unparalleled ability to communicate the truths of the Gospel. "The results of his preaching give irrefutable witness to its

---

[185]John A. Broadus, <u>On the Preparation and Delivery of Sermons</u> (San Francisco: Harper Collins, 1979), 3-4.

[186]Broadus, 7.

effectiveness."[187]   Paul referred to his preaching frequently and left no doubt that this was the thing that turned people to God (1 Corinthians 1:18-21). He referred to preaching fifty-three times in his epistles and described the call to preach as a significant milestone in his life (1 Timothy 2:7; 2 Timothy 1:11). It was the desire of Paul to see the next generation of ministers continue this emphasis on preaching (2 Timothy 4:2). "Thus the history of mission has been built on the preaching of God's Word,"[188] and God is still choosing to save men today through the "foolishness" of preaching.

It is imperative, therefore, that a missionary know how to preach.   Sadly, however, many missionaries are perceived as inadequate pulpiteers. They are seldom invited to speak at major preaching conferences, and the impression generally exists that missionaries have gone to the field because they are unable to hold an audience's attention at home.   There must be some objective criteria whereby the pulpit ministry of a missionary can be evaluated.

The Apostle Paul in the book of Philippians provided some criteria for this task (1:27-2:18). Here the reader finds "what Paul [expected] from the church."[189]   There existed some "wrong-headed thinking" in the Christian

---

[187]Dean S. Gilliland, Pauline Theology and Mission Practice (Eugene, OR: Wipf and Stock Publishers, 1998), 272.

[188]Gilliland, 272.

[189]Ralph P. Martin, The Epistle of Paul to the Philippians (Grand Rapids: Eerdmans Publishing Company, 1987), 84.

life, and it was the job of the preacher to correct it. This middle section in the book of Philippians is "firmly set within the framework of a pastoral exhortation," and therefore it is necessary "to see this entire section as a unity with no break."[190] In this sermon Paul articulated several key items that ought to be the focal point of a missionary's message.

Harmony in the Face of Pagan Influence

The Apostle Paul moved from a discussion of his hope of being reunited with the Philippians to a discussion of their being united among themselves. In so doing, he gave a stirring call and exhortation. He said that the inner life of the church must be considered, and that regardless of what else might happen, the Philippian church should conduct itself in a manner that becomes the Gospel of Christ (1:27).

The word μονον is placed emphatically at the beginning of the sentence structure indicating that this must happen "at all costs." The apostle had discussed his joyful spirit, but indicated that his spirit could be saddened if the Philippians failed to show themselves worthy of the Gospel of Christ. If they refused to live up to their heavenly citizenship, the incarcerated missionary would have been greatly disappointed. There is a standard of church life, and the believer must be exhorted to live up to it.

The distinctly Pauline phrase, "as becometh the Gospel,"[191] reminds the Christian that a very high standard of conduct is expected. "Christians have a high calling to

---

[190]Martin, 84.

[191]Romans 16:2; Ephesians 4:1; Colossians 1:10.

fulfill."[192] The privileges of the Christian life demand responsibility (Luke 12:48), and so the believer's behavior should reflect his thankfulness for the Gospel and be a visible proof that he has received the Gospel (1 John 3:18).

By using the verb πολιτενεσθε, Paul deliberately drew a parallel between the Christian community and the citizens of Rome. The Christian believer was to "live as a citizen" of Christ. Because Philippi was a Roman colony, the city was "intensely proud of its privileges."[193] The citizens of Philippi were treated as if they lived on Italian soil, and this was a cause for great civic pride (Acts 16:21). The Christians of Philippi, however, had a double allegiance. If it is true that a citizen of Rome had privileges to enjoy and responsibilities to fulfill, how much more is it true of one who is a citizen of Christ? The Philippian believers were not merely to accept the benefits of the Gospel; they were to accept the responsibilities of it as well. Just as the citizens of Philippi were to act as if they were on Italian soil, so the Christian is to act as if he is present in heaven.[194]

Paul states that this standard of Christian living should be implemented regardless of whether men are watching or not. The church was cautioned that it should not wait for Paul's return to put this principle into effect (1:27). Regardless of who was present, the Philippian believers needed to maintain their testimony through the practice of unity.

---

[192]Martin, 86.

[193]Martin, 86.

[194]Martin, 86-87.

They needed to "stand fast in one spirit" and "strive together" as fellow believers. Since the remainder of the verse states that this was to be done "in the Lord," it is entirely possible that the "one spirit" under discussion is the Holy Spirit rather than the Philippians' own disposition. As Martin well observes, however, "The Holy Spirit strengthens the human spirit," and thus "the two interpretations are not mutually exclusive."[195] The Holy Spirit of God unifies believers so that that they may fight together in a common spirit against pagan influences.

Thus, internal harmony is necessary to fight external pressure. The local church must contend as if it were one solitary individual. The verb συναθλουντες carries the connotation of war (2 Timothy 2:5) and was used of the gladiatorial struggles in the arena where life and death were hanging in the balance. Thus, the believers of Philippi were to be fighting side by side. Because of the issue at stake, unanimity was mandatory. Philip of Macedon used this tactical device of war when his spearmen fought in closed ranks. This was history with which the Philippians were familiar, and they were called to employ the same procedure in their combat against evil.[196]

In addition, the Philippians believers were to be of "one mind" (1:27), a reference to their inward disposition. If the church is weakened internally, it is not able to withstand external influences. A divided church can be a danger to itself, especially when adversaries are arriving on the scene. The Christian fight, then, is maintained on two

---

[195]Martin, 87.

[196]Martin, 88.

fronts. Externally, it is against the foe (1:28), and internally for unity around the faith of the Gospel (1:27).

"The faith" here seems to refer to the body of Christian truth, the faith that was once for all delivered to the saints (Jude 3). In days of persecution and doctrinal ambiguity the believer has no agreement unless there is agreement as to what constitutes "the faith." The missionary must always recognize that he presents in his preaching "a statement of facts, an assertion of things which can be understood, apprehended, accepted, disputed, or proved."[197] Surrounding paganism and false teaching must place the missionary on guard. There is a tendency today to avoid strong doctrine. The temptation exists to exaggerate the truth and virtue of heathen religions while minimizing the distinctiveness of Christianity. False religions are seldom seen as doctrinal error.[198]

As the missionary bears witness, he is not to be frightened by his opponents. The word πτυρομενοι (1:28) was used to denote an uncontrollable stampede of startled horses.[199] Those who distort the Gospel can frequently bring this fear, sometimes with mob violence. These adversaries, however, must not intimidate the believer.

When enmity is leveled against the believer, two things are immediately apparent: the perdition of the opponent and the salvation of the believer himself (1:28). Thus,

---

[197]Roland Allen, <u>Missionary Methods: St Paul's or Ours?</u> (Grand Rapids: Eerdmans Publishing Company, 1962), 63.

[198]Allen, 70.

[199]Martin, 89.

when the Christian is attacked, there is a double edge. "The suffering seals the doom of the persecutors as the enemies of the Gospel, and it confirms the eternal salvation of the faithful who endure to the end."[200] The persecution of the church is a great trial to faith, and yet it is "of God" (1:28). Why does God allow His people to be exposed to this persecution? At least part of the answer is that persecutions clearly help differentiate those who are in the faith from those who are not.

The sovereign control and purpose of God is to be seen throughout the persecution. This is the emphasis of verses 28 and 29. Suffering on behalf of Christ is something that has been "given" to us by God. There is, therefore, no accident in suffering. Suffering fulfills the purpose of God for His people in this world. The word translated "given" is derived from the word for "grace." So the Philippian believers were not only given the privilege of believing in Christ; they were also granted the privilege of suffering for Christ (1:29).

This suffering was something the Apostle Paul was privileged to do as well. Both the missionary and the church were called upon to suffer "the same conflict" (1:30). Believers, even though they may be separated by miles, often experience the same fight for the faith, the same kind of resistance, and the same grace through which they can conquer.[201] Thus, Paul's first major emphasis is that the Philippians must practice harmony in the face of pagan influence.

---

[200]Martin, 91.

[201]Martin, 93.

Paul was teaching the Philippian believers that when they became Christians they had not entered a solitary religious life, but a society in which the Spirit manifests Himself. It was inconceivable to the Apostle Paul that Christians entered a realm of independent salvation apart from participation with other believers,[202] and he knew that a failure to exercise harmonious relationships within the body would be at variance with the purpose of the Christian life.

Humility in the Face of Personal Ideologies

The word "therefore" that begins chapter two takes the reader back to 1:27. If the church is to be harmonious in the face of pagan influence, it must be humble in the face of personal ideologies. There can be no harmony in a church unless the members of that church are characterized by humility.

This humility is based on four certain realities. The word translated "if" is better rendered "since." To quote Martin, "Paul [had] no doubt that the matters on which he [grounded] his entreaty [were] definite realities in the experince of the Christians whom he [was] addressing."[203]

The first of these spiritual realities was "consolation in Christ" (2:1). The word παρακλησις is elsewhere translated "exhortation."[204] If this definition is adopted, the recipients were being given an apostolic authorization.

---

[202]Allen, 76.

[203]Martin, 93-94.

[204]Compare 1 Corinthians 14:3.

Thus, the first reason for humility is that Paul had given the church at Philippi an exhortation in Christ.

The second spiritual reality was the "comfort of love" (2:1). Christians are bound together in the household of faith by love. This "contraint of love" evidently refers to Christ's love for His church since the phrase looks back to the phrase "in Christ." Because the Philippians believers were constrained by the love of Christ for them, they should have been able to get along.

The third spiritual reality to which Paul referred was the "fellowship of the Spirit" (2:1). "Most commentators correctly understand 'spirit' as referring to the Holy Spirit rather than to the human spirit. But the more difficult problem to be resolved is: what is the meaning of the genitive phrase 'of the Spirit'?"[205] The main issue in interpreting the phrase is whether the genitive is subjective or objective. Martin convincingly argues that the genitive is objective and refers, not to the Spirit's creation of fellowship, but to the believer's possession of it. The phrase then refers to the readily acknowledged truth of the believer's participation in the Spirit.[206] Their common sharing in the Spirit should defeat all factiousness. Membership in the single body of Christ (Ephesians 4:4) is accomplished through the baptism of the Holy Spirit (1 Corinthians 12:13.) Such membership demands that all believers endeavor to keep the unity of

---

[205]Peter T. O'Brien, "The Fellowship Theme in Philippians," Reformed Theological Review 37, no. 1 (1978), 16.

[206]Martin, 50.

the Spirit (Ephesians 4:3). "This is the basic theological foundation of all Christian unity."[207]

The final spiritual reality that Paul mentioned was "bowels and mercies" (2:1). The term σπλαγχνα refers to the "viscera as the emotional state," while the term οικτιρμοι signifies "the outward expression of deep feeling in passionate yearning and action."[208] Thus Paul grounded his appeal for humility on the power of sympathy.

The appeal for humility, then, is not merely a piece of superficial advice. Instead, Paul's appeal is motivated by Christ's will, constrained by Christ's love, founded in believers' mutual participation in the Spirit, and enhanced by the qualities of kindness and sympathy that believers ought to feel for one another. When division is threatening the fellowship and marring the testimony of a local church, these four profound truths are worth remembering.

The Apostle Paul's joy would be complete if these truths were remembered and acted upon. The joy of the missioanry comes by seeing his converts "likeminded, having the same love, being of one accord, of one mind" (2:2). This "piling up" of expressions was intentional. There can be no doubt as to Paul's desire for them. Because they shared a common outlook, unity and amity must prevail.

This can be done, however, only when selfish ambition is set aside. Martin suggests that the word εριθειαν be

---

[207]Martin, 95.

[208]Martin, 95.

translated "quarrelsomeness."[209] By his own admonition, however, this suggestion does not contain the hint of self-seeking normally associated with the word. The Philippian believers were not to let anything be done through selfish ambition that would reveal a heart of vain conceit. Factiousness and vanity were the evils that plagued the Christian community at Philippi, and the only antidote was a good dose of humility.

Humility begins with a recognition of one's dependence upon God and one's true condition in God's sight. This humility before God leads to a humility in one's relations with other people.[210] The person who possesses such humility will be aware of his own weaknesses, and consequently he will esteem others better than himself (2:3).

This should be the aim of the Christian life. Paul's use of the word σκοπειτε suggests that the good points and qualities in one's fellow believers be looked for, recognized, and emulated (2:4). This, of course, prepares the way for a close examination of the Lord's example in verses five through eleven. Egocentric demeanors and haughty attitudes can destroy the fellowship in a church. The believer then must not be preoccupied with his own life to the degree that he misses positive traits in others.

The missionary speaker must encourage others to examine the excellencies of others, particularly the excellencies of Christ. He must not only encourage his audience to be harmonious in the face of pagan influences;

---

[209]Martin, 96.

[210]Martin, 97.

he must also encourage them to be humble in the face of personal ideologies.

A Powerful Illustration

The Philippians were then challenged with the greatest possible incentive to harmony and humility in the picture of the Lord Himself whose attitude is described in the great verses that follow (2:5-11). Paul showed that believers must share the spirit of their Lord and be controlled by the pattern of His humility that was exemplified in the incarnation and the cross.[211]

The Christian preacher is limited when he takes his examples from the realm of fallen men. There is, however, a model for imitation that supersedes the sphere of sinful creatures. The preacher has the supreme privilege of pointing men to the unparalleled Christ. When the Christian life is evaluated, it is only fair to look at Jesus. The mere mention of His name is a powerful enough incentive for the abandonment of every attitude that would do Him violence. The preacher is always on solid ground when He points men to the Savior.[212]

Such was the preaching nature of Paul. His preaching showed a remarkable ability to keep Jesus Christ central, especially His atoning death and bodily resurrection. "The emphasis on the death of Christ that appears throughout the epistles assumes that a considerable amount of preaching and teaching of the life of Jesus has

---

[211]Martin, 99-100.

[212]M. Rhodes, Expository Lectures on Philippians (Philadelphia: Lutheran Publication Society, 1882), 121-22. .

already taken place."[213] References to the cross abound in Paul's letters. To quote the famous missionary, "We preach Christ" (1 Corinthians 1:23). This was the thing that unified Paul's converts. "Where the mind of Christ is, there will be unity"[214] (2:5).

Christ Jesus was "in the form of God" (2:6). "The phrase looks back to our Lord's pre-temporal existence as the second person of the trinity."[215] The apostle was not speaking of His external appearance, but of His essential attributes and nature. "The Son is one in nature, one in attributes, one in character with the Father."[216] If the Philippian believers thought they were superior because of their Roman citizenship, how much more superior was the Son of God? If any person had a right to consider himself, it was Jesus Christ. He was "in the form of God" and "equal with God."

Jesus, however, did not consider this position something at which to grasp. "He existed in the divine condition or rank as the unique image and glory of God, but refused to utilize this favored position to exploit His privileges and assert Himself in opposition to His Father."[217] The word αρπαγμον here refers to the holding of a privilege that can be exploited for profit by the

---

[213]Gilliland, 274.

[214]Rhodes, 127.

[215]Martin, 100.

[216]J. Dwight Pentecost, The Joy of Living (Grand Rapids: Zondervan Publishing House, 1973), 67.

[217]Martin, 102-103.

possessor. In His pre-existent state Jesus already had as His possession a unique dignity and place within the Godhead. From this unique position Christ could have asserted His rights and seized glory and honor. At this point, however, Christ made a choice to resist glory and honor in this way. He chose to be proclaimed equal with God as "the Lord" by accepting His destiny as a servant.[218]

Because He did not regard His equality with God as a treasure to be clutched and retained at all costs, Christ emptied Himself. The phrase εαυτον εκενωσε is best interpreted in light of the words that immediately follow. The verse teaches that Christ's "kenosis" was His taking the servant's form.[219] Christ, however, was not completely divested of His glory. This is evidenced by our Lord's transfiguration in the presence of Peter, James, and John. They were permitted to see the glory of God that was still present in Jesus, although it had been veiled by human flesh. The idea, then, is that Christ's glory was limited voluntarily in the incarnation. "He divested Himself of the prerogatives of deity, but His essential person was not changed."[220]

Though more recent exegetes tend to disagree, "the form of a servant" (2:7) is a vivid description of Christ's humanity. He shared the frailties and finitude of human nature. He was "circumscribed by the restrictions imposed by that nature with the glorious exception that He

---

[218]Martin, 103.

[219]Martin, 104.

[220]Martin, 103.

was without sin."[221] His true status was concealed and veiled in His humanity.

A servant is characterized by a lack of rights. A servant submits himself to the will of the master. In this passage Paul emphasized that Jesus came into the world as one who had no rights. All the rights that belonged to the Son of God were laid aside and not used. He divested Himself of the voluntary use of those attributes and qualities so that He might be subject to another. It was the supreme demonstration of harmony and humility. When Jesus Christ came into the world, He did so, not to do His own will, but the will of another (Hebrews 10:7). He set aside His own will to submit Himself totally and completely to the will of the Father. He was humbling Himself.[222]

Our Lord became fully man (2:8) in order that He might humble Himself and become obedient. This was the example that Christ set for the believer, and even the proud Greeks who considered humility a contemptuous thing were commanded to accept it. If any man feels that he cannot humble himself because of his position in life, he needs to consider Jesus Christ. The mind of Christ does not acknowledge one's rights, but delights to set aside those rights for the good of another.[223]

In the case of Christ, this humbling obedience culminated in His passion and death at Calvary. Thus "His obedience is a sure token of His deity and authority

---

[221]Martin, 105.

[222]Pentecost, 69.

[223]Pentecost, 70-71.

for only a divine being can accept" the fact of "death as obedience; for ordinary people it is a necessity."[224] No other man has a choice about the eventuality of death. Jesus alone could choose death as His destiny, and this was done for the sake of obedience (Hebrews 10:7). The words "even the death of the cross" demonstrate the depths to which He was prepared to go in obedience; they signify the utter limit of His humiliation.

This form of capital punishment repulsed residents of a Roman city such as Philippi. Death by crucifixion was the most cruel and hideous form of punishment. Cicero stated that Roman citizens should not experience it with their thoughts, eyes, or ears, much less their bodies.[225]

In addition, Jews understood crucifixion to place one outside the pale of Israel (Deuteronomy 21:23). Anyone who experienced crucifixion was considered excommunicated from God's covenant. This thought proved to be a stumbling block to many Jewish people (1 Corinthians 1:23).[226] Thus Paul brought the reader from the highest height to the lowest depth.

Because Christ, however, was willing to take obedience to this extreme, the Father raised His Son from the dead and elevated Him to a place of honor (2:9). The resurrection and exaltation of Christ are the Father's response to the absolute obedience of His Son. This

---

[224]Martin, 106-107.

[225]Martin, 107.

[226]Martin, 107.

principle of exaltation following humiliation is found throughout the entire Bible.[227]

The Christ who stooped so low was gloriously lifted up. He is now able to enjoy the dignity that was always His by right. Because He did not clutch at this glory as His personal possession, glory is ascribed to Him. He has obtained it through submission and sacrifice. Honor is now conferred upon Him because He chose not to assume it by right or seizure. Instead, this honor is bestowed upon Him by the Father's good pleasure (2:9).[228]

Thus, the human name "Jesus" is important because it declares that lordly power has been committed to the hands of the historical person of Jesus of Nazareth. He has been given the supreme name of "Lord." This was the word that was used in the LXX to translate the divine name of Jehovah. "In view of this special connotation with the name of God in the Old Testament the giving of the name in this context declares that Jesus Christ is installed in the place which properly belongs to God Himself as Lord of all creation."[229]

Because this is true, two outstanding things will happen. At the name of Jesus every knee must bow (2:10), and every tongue must confess that Jesus Christ is Lord (2:11). Both of these affirmations find their origin in Isaiah 45:22-23 where the uniqueness of Israel's God is stressed. The Old Testament quotation used in reference

---

[227]Matthew 18:4; 23:12; Luke 4:11; 18:14; 2 Corinthians 11:7; Philippians 4:12.

[228]Martin, 108-109.

[229]Martin, 109.

to the exclusive God is now used in reference to Jesus Christ. There could be no clearer proof of the Lord's pre-eminent position.[230]

Heavenly begins, earthly beings, and infernal beings will recognize his universal authority. Though the King James Version takes the adjectives as a reference to implied neuter nouns, the reference here is not to "things." The reference is personal and applies to intelligent beings whether they are in heaven, or in earth, or in the underworld. All will bend the knee in submission to the One who was the pattern of submission, and will echo the creed of Christianity down through the centuries — Jesus Christ is Lord.[231] Thus, Paul portrays the Lord Jesus Christ as the supreme example of harmony and humility, an example that is worthy of emulation.

A Passionate Invitation

The Apostle Paul, having argued for harmony (1:27-30) and humility (2:1-4), and having portrayed Christ as the supreme example of both (2:5-11), now begins to make application (2:12-18). The term "wherefore" (2:12) connects what the Lord has done with what the believer should do. Because Jesus obeyed, the believer should obey, and because Jesus is Lord, the believer should live under His rule.[232]

As Paul made this application, he did so with a pastor's heart. He addressed the Philippian believers as "my

---

[230]Martin, 109.

[231]Martin, 110.

[232]Martin, 114.

beloved" (2:12). This is not necessarily to soften the exhortation, but to remind the Christians to whom he was writing that this appeal was a loving expression. The commands of Paul, like the commands of Christ, were not meant to be grievous (I John 5:3).

Indeed, the Philippian church had a "track record" of obedience, and the missionary anticipated that this reputation would continue. Paul expected this obedience to continue not only when apostolic authority was present, but when it was absent as well. Regardless of what human authorities might have been watching, he expected the Philippian believers to "work out" their "own salvation" (2:12).

From the context, however, it seems clear that this mentioned salvation was not their personal salvation in Jesus Christ. The entire sermon of Paul, which began in 1:27, has centered on the fellowship within the Philippian church. The message has encouraged the believers at Philippi to work at restoring church unity. "Salvation," then, is referring to the salvation of "spiritual health in the community," which has been "diseased by strife and bad feeling."[233] This is a legitimate use for the word σωτηριαν. For example, the word is translated "health" in Acts 27:34 because it refers to the "salvation" of one's body. At Philippi the "health" of Christ's body was at stake.

The words "your own," therefore, cannot be taken in a personal sense, especially since the apostle had just warned them not to focus on their own individual matters (2:4). The reference must look back to the opening words of the sermon (1:28) where the "salvation" of the entire

---

[233]Martin, 115.

church was in view. The context of the entire sermon demands this interpretation. After the great truth of Christ's humility and sacrifice of personal rights, it would be inappropriate to stress personal salvation. Christ did not save Himself personally in order that the corporate body might be saved. The reader must, therefore, take the words of Paul to refer to "the attitude of the Philippians towards one another in the fellowship of the church."[234]

This spirit is one of humility. The words "fear and trembling" (2:12) are used elsewhere by Paul to describe the believer's attitude toward men.[235] This spirit of humility should characterize the mutual relationships of the Philippian believers.

This would not be done, however, apart from the power of God. They could only work out this salvation of corporate unity because God worked among them and was in the midst. The term ενεργων denotes effective working. God produced both "the will to amend the condition of His people and [brought] about the accomplishment of this state of goodwill in their midst."[236] The phrase "of His good pleasure" (2:13) should not be taken to refer to God's goodwill expressed toward the Philippians, but to "the pattern of goodwill which His gracious activity promotes in the fellowship as He inspires the will and energizes the achievement of amicable relationships."[237] While it is true that the

---

[234]Martin, 116.

[235]2 Corinthians 7:15; Ephesians 6:5.

[236]Martin, 116-17.

[237]Martin, 117.

word ευδοκιας can refer to the will of God who shows His "good pleasure" by blessing His people, it can equally refer to human goodwill (1:15), and that is the sense here. Paul expected goodwill to characterize the believing community at Philippi, and that was only possible because God as at work in their midst.

That the "salvation" under discussion was social rather than personal is confirmed by verse 14, where they are indicted for murmuring and disputing. Thus, we understand that the "strife and vainglory" (2:3) of the Philippian believers was beginning to manifest itself in complaining and arguing against each other. This was the root evil in the heart of the church.

This lack of harmony and humility was hindering their testimony, so the apostle sounded a call to "amendment and improvement." He said the church must rid itself of selfish ambition and vain conceit so that it could be "blameless and harmless" (2:15). The first term, αμεμπτοι, means "irreproachable, living a life at which no finger can be pointed." The second term, ακεραιοι, was employed in first-century literature of "wine that was undiluted or metals that contain no weakening alloy."[238]

The Philippians in their character and their conduct were to live so that no outsider could pass valid criticism on their public behavior. Simultaneously, "there should be no foreign element that [intruded] and [undermined] their strength or [contaminated] the church's real nature as a pure virgin."[239] In the words "blameless and harmless" there was a fitting commentary on what it means to live

---

[238]Martin, 118.

[239]Martin, 119.

as one who "becomes the Gospel of Christ" (1:27). The invitation of Paul practically suggests how the Philippian believers may live according to his opening injunction.

Because his Philippian readers were "the sons of God" (2:15), they were to live "without rebuke" in spite of the fact that they lived "in the midst of a crooked and perverse nation." The terminology took the reader back to Deuteronomy 32:5 where Israel was reprimanded for her apostasy, but when Paul adopted the terms from this Old Testament passage, he also adapted them. The Philippian believers could not be spoken of as a "crooked and perverse nation" in spite of their murmuring and disputing with one another. They were still "the sons of God." So while the words "crooked and perverse nation" were used in Deuteronomy of erring Israel, Paul applied them here to the surrounding world in which the Philippian church was to witness.[240]

It is important to note that the task of witnessing takes place "in the midst" of such a world. Though believers are not a part of this present world's evil system, they still live among the people of this world. This is part of God's will (John 17:15-16). Christians are not to withdraw as recluses, but are commissioned to go into the very world from which they have been redeemed (John 17:18). It is always proper for the Christian to be in the world, for only here can he have an influence and bear a witness for Christ.[241]

---

[240]Martin, 119-20.

[241]Martin, 120.

Paul described the world as a dark place in need of light. Christians are the vessels through whom the light of God is manifested. Those who are children of God are also children of the light (1 Thessalonians 5:5). This light of God is manifested when believers hold forth "the word of life" (2:16). The verb επεχοντες can mean "to hold fast or firmly" or "to hold out, offer."[242] It seems best in this context to interpret the word as the King James translators did when they rendered the word "holding forth." The Philippian believers, through a consistent testimony, had a golden opportunity to share the light of Christ in a dark world. Rather than being frightened into silence (1:28), the Philippian believers were exhorted to let their light shine.

Any failure to do this would have kept Paul from rejoicing "in the day of Christ" (2:16). He would not rejoice because the apostolic care he had invested on them would have been for naught. In such a case Paul would have "run in vain." The terminology took the reader to the stadium where a runner learns that he has been disqualified as he completes his course. He, therefore, has exerted himself for nothing. Similarly, the words "labored in vain" were taken from the field of weaving when a piece of cloth was rejected because it was badly woven. There would be no payment for the cloth, and the labor would have been in vain. The apostle wanted to experience no such disappointment in the field of missionary service. He wanted to finish his course with joy because his work had "passed the test." He wanted to be rewarded in the day of Christ for a job well done.[243]

---

[242]Martin, 121.

[243]Martin, 122.

The metaphors of athletic competition and weaving soon give way to the example of sacrifice. Paul was ready to "be offered" (2:17). The verb means "to pour out as a drink offering and denotes, in sacrificial terms, a violent, even a bloody death."[244] His life-blood that would be shed in death is likened to a libation in a sacrificial ritual. The fact that the verb is in the present tense indicates that the possibility of martyrdom was very vivid in the apostle's mind.

Although Paul mentioned his own death, the significant part of the sacrificial ritual is the faith of the Philippian believers. "Paul's libation would not be complete without that and this act of sacrifice is the main feature of the sentence."[245] The Christians at Philippi were offering their faith by their active support of the missionary's needs. Their gifts, which were sent to him out of poverty, were a sacrificial service that rose as an acceptable offering to God.[246] The Philippian church was exercising a priestly ministry of service. "Their faith, which was made visible and evident in the gifts which they had sacrificially contributed and which gave them a share in Paul's affliction, [were] the sacrifice. Paul's life-blood, to be shed in martyrdom for Christ, [was] the accompanying libation."[247]

As Paul viewed the prospect of martyrdom, however, he was not discouraged. On the contrary, he was joyful.

---

[244]Martin, 123.

[245]Martin, 123.

[246]See Philippians 4:14, 18.

[247]Martin, 124.

The reader had already learned that this joy was based on the fact that death would be gain (1:21). Thus, Paul rejoiced in the prospect of martyrdom and with the Philippian believers in their sacrifice on his behalf.

The phrase το δε αυτο και (2:18) was a call to the Philippians to receive this news with gladness and to share his joy. The prefix of the verb "rejoice," συγχαιρω in verse 17, and συγχαιρετε in verse 18, is the preposition of united experience. It was used to stress the importance of unity within the church as all divisions ceased (1:27). There was a close bond between the apostle and the church, and the Philippian believers had proven that the link between Paul and them was reciprocal.[248] The Philippian church, then, was capable of harmonious and humble relationships. The church demonstrated these relationship in its relationship to the Apostle Paul. Now the church is being challenged to demonstrate them in relationship to each other.

Humility and the Missionary Candidate

When Paul exhorted the Philippian believers to harmony and humility through the example of Christ, he expected results. Paul's invitation was fervent because he fully anticipated that the Philippians would follow his dictates and restore proper fellowship to their divided assembly. There is a lesson here for the missionary candidate.

In spite of the fact that the Philippians could have rejected Paul's message, he did not hesitate to preach it. "He [did] not apologize for it, he [did] not attmept to

---

[248]Martin, 125.

conceal its weight. He [set] it forth definitely, clearly, boldly."[249]

The whole while, Paul expected his hearers to be moved. He believed in his preaching, and this was a very significant part of his presentation. He had faith that his listeners would respond. As Allen so aptly states, "A mere preaching which is not accompanied by the expectation of faith, is not true preaching."[250] If the seed is merely scattered with a vague hope that some of it may sprout, true preaching has not occurred. Preachers should believe that they have been sent to those who are being addressed at that moment. The one who is delivering the message should expect a response; this is why an air of expectation pervaded the preaching of the Apostle Paul. This is why people were afraid of his preaching; something was expected to come of it.

In addition, the preaching of this missionary was designed to bring his audience to a point. The exhortations of Paul were never indeterminate and inconclusive. Paul was not interested in talking to village after village with no results. "Paul did not scatter seeds, he planted."[251] He always sought to bring his listeners to a speedy and direct point of decision. He demanded that they make a choice and act upon it. Moral issues were clearly presented, and the thought ran throughout that the missionary was not merely presenting novel and interesting ideas; he was mandating a way of life.

---

[249]Allen, 63.

[250]Allen, 74.

[251]Allen, 74.

This, of course, meant that rejection was a distinct possibility. Paul, however, would not establish himself in a place indefinitely if those people refused to act on his teaching (Acts 18:6). He openly rejected those who rejected his teaching. Allen goes so far as to argue that Biblical truth cannot be properly presented if this element is left out. "Can there be a true teaching which does not involve the refusal to go on teaching?"[252] The true preacher cannot be interested in the education of the intellect only. He must be involved in a moral process and must demand a moral response.

Should missionaries plant themselves in towns or villages and continue for years when the people to whom they are preaching have no inclination to obey? The same Lord who issued the command to go also issued the command to shake the dust off one's feet (Matthew 10:14).

Do today's missionaries have the courage to address their supporting churches as Paul did here in Philippians 1:27-2:18? Is the missionary on deputation so concerned about financial backing that he preaches without demanding a verdict? Paul was thankful for the sacrifice that the Philippians had made on his behalf (2:17), but this did not prevent him from demanding that they stop their murmuring and disputing (2:14). In their zeal to offend no one, perhaps missionaries on deputation have blessed no one through straightforward, verdict-demanding sermons.

---

[252]Allen, 75.

Chapter 7
Vision for the Future

To be a successful missionary one must have a vision for the future, and this necessitates the establishment of goals. Many missionaries, however, are satisfied with general statements of purpose that are little more than platitudes. Such statements of ambiguity fail to help the missionary evaluate whether he is doing his job appropriately. "A goal must be measurable or it is of no functional value."[253] Unfortunately, such goals are frequently absent in the missionary enterprise. Lud Golz, for example, states, "After visiting missionaries on a number of fields over the past few years, I've come away dismayed because far too many of them have only a vague idea about what they're supposed to be doing."[254] It is not always easy to state goals in precise terms, but a serious attempt must be made to do so, for it is not possible to determine strategy unless one possesses well-thought-out goals.[255] God's servants have no choice but to "measure the effectiveness of their efforts and evaluate the significance of what is learned for future planning."[256]

---

[253]James F. Engel and William Norton, What's Gone Wrong with the Harvest? (Grand Rapids: Zondervan Publishing House, 1975), 89-90.

[254]Lud Golz, "If Paul Got Organized to Reach His Objectives, So Can You," Evangelical Missions Quarterly 27, no. 3 (1991), 268.

[255]Engel and Norton, 124.

[256]Engel and Norton, 100.

How, then, is one to plan for the future? Paul, the great missionary, once again provides helpful hints. The more one considers this problem in the light of Scripture, the more he will be convinced that much can be learned from the Apostle Paul. "He knew how to manage life and ministry with a view toward finishing the race."[257] In the book of Philippians (2:19-30) the apostle gives four practical principles on how to face the future with vision.

Vision Necessitates Planning

The subject matter of the Philippian letter changed in the middle of chapter two as Paul expressed his hopes for the future. These plans "denote what Paul had in intention, notably his desire to visit his congregations as a follow-up to his letters."[258] The word "but" (2:19) provides a link back to verse 12. Paul had already mentioned that his absence from the Philippian believers was unavoidable because of his incarceration. Nevertheless, Paul was concerned about the Philippian believers. Thus, he would send Timothy who was with him at the time as an envoy and representative. Paul hoped that Timothy would return from the Philippian church with a satisfactory report that would prove to be "of good comfort" to the apostle. The mission of Timothy, therefore, must be understood in terms of Paul's appeal for unity in the Philippian church.[259] Timothy was to report back to Paul as to whether his apostolic

---

[257]Golz, 268.

[258]Ralph P. Martin, <u>The Epistle of Paul to the Philippians</u> (Grand Rapids: Eerdman's Publishing Company, 1987), 126.

[259]Martin, 126.

injunctions had been obeyed. Paul was planning to evaluate the progress of the Philippians by sending Timothy.

Paul not only had the future goal of sending Timothy (2:23), he also had an immediate plan to send Epaphroditus (2:25). Many commentators assume that Epaphroditus was the bearer of the Philippian letter. If this is true, the phrase "I supposed it necessary to send" should be taken as an epistolary aorist. In other words, Paul was placing himself in the position of his readers. By the time they received the letter, Paul's actions and thoughts would have already occurred.[160] By using this device, Paul revealed to the Philippians his planning process.

These plans are further amplified in verse 28 where Paul stated that he sent Epaphroditus very eagerly. The adverb σπουδαιοτέρως is best rendered as a superlative. Paul was extremely excited that Epaphroditus was being sent back to Philippi, and wanted the Philippian believers to share in this excitement.

Paul's commendation is inserted to avoid any criticism against Epaphroditus for his return. The Apostle Paul made it clear that he accepted full responsibility for this decision (2:25). The Philippian believers may have been disappointed and assumed that their sending of Epaphroditus to Paul to minister to the apostle's needs was a failed venture. The Philippians could have easily assumed that Paul was without sympathy and friendship due to the departure of Epaphroditus. Paul answered that criticism in advance by praising the return of this man. He told the Philippian church why Epaphroditus had come

---

[160]Martin, 133.

home. These words should have quieted any criticism and led to gladness over his restored health and presence.[261]

The sorrow of Paul's incarceration would have been intensified if the Philippian believers had treated Epaphroditus unkindly (2:28). It was right for him to return home, not as a deserter and a weakling, but as one who had been providentially orchestrated to be in Philippi. The Philippian church was to accept his return with joy because God had mandated it.

Paul said that he should be received "in the Lord with all gladness" (2:29). The believers were to resist the temptation to misunderstand the motives and malign the actions of Epaphroditus. Rather, they were to have a Christ-like attitude of reception, demonstrating that love always believes the best (1 Corinthians 13:7). Epaphroditus was an honorable man, and honorable men should be treated as such.[262] These words show how Paul planned for the return of Epaphroditus. Paul was able to see potential problems and plan accordingly. This is a valuable lesson for all missionaries.

"Paul carefully wove his future plans into his report on what he had done and was doing."[263] When Luke recorded the missionary activity of Paul in the book of Acts, it became self-evident that Paul had a strategy. All of the cities or towns where Paul planted churches were centers of Roman administration, Greek civilization,

---

[261]Martin, 136

[262]Martin, 136-37.

[263]Golz, 269.

Jewish influence, and commerical importance.[264] Lystra and Derbe were military posts where there was a strong Roman element. Lystra was obviously a center of Greek civilization, for half the inscriptions that have been discovered there are Greek. Most of the places where Paul established churches were also centers of Jewish influence, as evidenced by the vast number of synagogues in which Paul preached. In addition, these cities were strategic centers of world commerce. It is clear from Luke's account that Paul put planning and thought into every policy decision. Paul "seized strategic points because he had a strategy."[265]

The book of Philippians reveals that Paul did not limit his planning to church planting endeavors. When he issued an order, he planned for someone like Timothy to follow up on its accomplishment. When correspondence was written, he planned for its distribution. When colleagues were meeting, he planned for a smooth encounter. Paul's entire missionary life was marked by forethought. To quote Hiebert, "In a rational orderly world it is possible to plan for the future — to set goals and achieve them, to see problems and forestall them. It is important, therefore, to plan ahead."[266]

To a large degree missionaries are made or broken by the choices they make. Human beings have the power of

---

[264]Roland Allen, Missionary Methods: Paul's or Ours? (Grand Rapids: Eerdmans Publishing Company, 1962), 13.

[265]Allen, 17.

[266]Paul Hiebert, Anthropological Insights for Missionaries (Grand Rapids: Baker Book House, 1987), 119.

choice, and this carries with it the weight of responsibility. Anyone who desires to succeed in the future must be characterized by sane, rational decisions, and this mandates proper planning.

Vision Utilizes People

Proper planning cannot be done, however, without the using of people. This is why Paul's vision for the future included two of his most trusted friends: Timothy and Epaphroditus.

Timothy frequently functioned as Paul's personal representative to local churches,[267] and it is as a trusted colleague that Timothy is commended here (2:20). Paul states that there was "no man like-minded." The word ισοψυχον literally means "of equal soul" and is used in the LXX of Psalm 55:13 to denote the equality that exists in close human friendship. Thus Timothy was placed in a very high position of honor as an intimate friend. No one among Paul's current inner circle (4:21-22) cared more for the Philippians than Timothy. No one had the same spirit as Timothy toward the Philippian church, and this made Timothy the likely candidate to be sent. He had a genuine interest in the church's spiritual state. Just as Timothy had been "genuine" in his relationship with the apostle (1 Timothy 1:2), so he had been "genuine" in his relationship with the Philippians; the term γνησιως is used in both verses. The concern that the Apostle Paul had for all the churches (2 Corinthians 11:28) was shared by Timothy for the church at Philippi.[268]

---

[267]1 Corinthians 4:17; 16:10; 1 Thessalonians 3:2.

[268]Martin, 127-28.

Paul recognized that in a world of selfishness it is rare to find a man like Timothy. He was always ready to promote the welfare of other people and to give himself to a weary journey so that personal quarrels in a local church might be solved (2:21). Paul knew that the divisions in the Philippian church would be difficult to handle and that the one who was chosen to go there must possess "tact, wisdom, and patience."[269] Timothy was a young man (1 Timothy 4:12), a physically weak man (1 Timothy 5:23), and a reserved man by nature (1 Corinthians 16:10). He was, however, chosen by Paul. This choice speaks well of Timothy's readiness to help, and also of Paul's ability to delegate to people who were naturally less qualified than he was.

Many missionaries have experienced betrayal, and this is unpleasant. In working with other believers, the evangelist frequently experiences disappointment. Trusted workers sometimes "run off" with the money. The missionary, however, must not become suspicious of everyone. If he does, no one will have the opportunity to prove himself trustworthy. Even Paul was not able to avoid the pitfall of choosing a companion who turned out wrong (2 Timothy 4:10). It is hard for the missionary to forget the shame of having been fooled by someone, but this must occur, for only in this way will the untrustworthy learn trustworthiness. If this is not done, the worthy ones will have no chance to prove themselves worthy. If the missionary withdraws in fears and doubts, he will never know who will make a true friend.[270]

---

[269]Martin, 130.

[270]Joseph L. Cannon, <u>For Missionaries Only</u> (Grand Rapids: Baker Book House, 1969), 59.

Paul was known for taking men into confidence in order that they might be approved (2:22). Timothy was given a chance to show himself to be a man of character and worth. He was placed in a position where there was a chance to stand (Acts 16). Timothy was given the opportunity to be tested and proved.

This happened because Paul was willing to treat him as a son, a comparison frequently employed by Paul.[271] "Paul was Timothy's father in the Gospel, leading him to Christ and fostering him in the things of the Lord."[272] This relationship[273] afforded Timothy the opportunity to serve with the Apostle Paul in the extension of the Gospel. Rather than viewing himself as a superior, Paul was yoked together with Timothy in common service for the single cause of the Gospel. Both men functioned like their Savior and took the form of a servant (2:7).

Paul's attitude toward Timothy was also manifested toward Epaphroditus (2:25). Paul viewed him as a fellow believer, fellow worker, and fellow soldier. The two men were in the same family and the same work, and they experienced the same camaraderie.[274]

Paul allowed Epaphroditus to work close to him, and this produced the opportunity for him to become a valued

---

[271] 1 Corinthians 4:14-15; Philemon 10; Galatians 4:19, 1 Thessalonians 2:11.

[272] Martin, 130.

[273] Acts 16:1-3; 1 Timothy 4:14; 2 Timothy 1:6; 1 Corinthians 4:17.

[274] Martin, 133.

colleague. Epaphroditus became an "apostle" in his own right to the church at Philippi. He did this by bringing the financial gifts of the Philippian church to the incarcerated apostle. Epaphroditus, however, had not intended to bring money only. It was his intention to stay indefinitely as a companion to Paul.

Epaphroditus was concerned with ministry. The word λειτουργον was used in first-century literature to convey associations of sacred and solemn work undertaken for religious purposes.[275] There is a special solemnity, then, associated with the work of Epaphroditus. His work was rendered, not only to Paul, but also to the Lord.

Epaphroditus was so serious in this work for Christ that he nearly worked himself to death (2:30). The fact that he did not regard his own life as precious is a rebuke to many who are satisfied with an easy-going Christianity. Epaphroditus placed stern demands upon himself and was characterized by self-denial. He gave little thought to his own personal comfort and safety as he discharged his responsibilities.[276] The plans of the missionary always included people.

This act of self-denial made up for the Philippian church's "lack of service." A parallel is found 1 Corinthians 16:17 where Stephanas, Fortunatus, and Achaicus made up the absence of the Corinthians. Epaphroditus labored side by side with the Apostle

---

[275]Martin, 134.

[276]Martin, 137-38.

Paul.[277]   The plans of the missionary always included people.

Vision Initiates Performance

In addition to mandating planning and using people, vision initiates performance. After the commendation of Timothy, Paul expressed his hope that he would be able to send Timothy soon (2:23). As soon as Paul was able to ascertain the outcome of his detention, he would send Timothy to them to communicate news of Paul's condemnation or release.[278]   Paul made plans. These plans included people. Once these plans were formulated, they were implemented. A proper vision always initiates action.

Paul "found a way to maintain discipline to do what God wanted him to do"[279] Paul's objectives were always measurable. Herein lies the reason for having a clearly defined purpose statement. If the missionary does not know what his purpose is, he will have a difficult time maintaining discipline in his life and work. "Having established his purpose, Paul broke it down into goal statements, so that he could rank his activities."[280]   His objectives were precise enough so that he could check them off as they were done.

---

[277]Martin, 138.

[278]Martin, 131.

[279]Golz, 270.

[280]Golz, 270.

Often missionary teams state that their purpose is to plant a church. Frequently, however, there are no measurable goals established to accomplish this task. With no measurable goals in place, these teams find it difficult to maintain discipline and stay on target. How can a progress report be written if the missionary does not have measurable steps toward achieving a specific goal?[281]

All too often the missionary becomes troubled and worried because he has not prioritized his schedule and functioned according to those priorities. "Though he may be busy doing many good things, he fails to perform"[282] in the areas that are most important. Often this results in fatigue and illness that, in the long run, hinder missionary productivity. "A person who is placed in unusually frustrating and unpredictable circumstances where his goals are not easily met, will experience anxiety, fear and hostility."[283] It is imperative, then, that a missionary "plan his work" and then "work his plan." A failure to plan results in a failure to perform. Vision initiates performance.

Vision Recognizes Providence

As the Apostle Paul made the people-oriented plans that he intended to perform, intellectual reasoning was not

---

[281]Golz, 271.

[282]Cannon, 55.

[283]Kelly S. O'Donnell and Michele Lewis O'Donnell, eds., Helping Missionaries Grow (Pasadena, CA: William Carey Library, 1988), 353.

[284]Allen, 16.

his only methodology. Paul was able to recognize the providence of God in every situation. He was led of the Spirit[284] and recognized when it was necessary to alter his plans so that the plan of God might be done. The outcome of Paul's incarceration was uncertain, and therefore, whatever plans Paul made, they had to be "in the Lord" (2:24). This "holy hesitation" was directly attributable to Paul's reliance upon divine providence. "If he had any assurance of a happy issue out of his troubles it [was] only in submission to the divine will, and therefore 'in the Lord' may be the equivalent of 'if the Lord is willing' as in 1 Corinthians 4:19."[285]

His reliance upon the providence of God is also seen in reference to Epaphroditus (2:26). The fine plans of the Philippians to send Epaphroditus to Paul in order that he might permanently minister to the apostle's needs had gone awry. Epaphroditus had fallen sick, and somehow the news of his sickness had traveled back to Philippi. From there came a report to Paul that the Philippians were concerned about him. This, in turn, caused Epaphroditus to "long after" the Philippians and to be "full of heaviness." The first term, επιποθων, was used previously of Paul's ardent desire to see the Philippians once more. The second term, αδημονων, was used to describe the Lord's agony in Gethsemane (Matthew 26:37; Mark 14:33) and denotes great perturbation.[286] For these reasons, Paul submitted to the providence of God and sent Epaphroditus back to the Philippians regardless of what previous plans had determined.

---

[285]Martin, 132.

[286]Martin, 134.

It is not surprising that Kane lists "adaptability" as one of the major psychological qualifications for a missionary.[287] The missionary must plan to use people. He must also have a desire to perform the plans that have been formulated, but he must always understand that the Lord has the prerogative to change these plans. His providence can overrule.

As Cannon rightly states, "Plans need to be made, and God-given talents used, but we had better keep our ears tuned to God's providence."[288] Paul had his own ideas, but he always "gave" the Lord the "chance to disagree." Men of God are always guided by the Holy Spirit, and, in the final analysis, they must do what God desires regardless of natural inclinations. Christians in general, and missionaries in particular, can become filled with self-importance. Because Christ is the Head of the church, His will is to be done. It is imperative, therefore, that a missionary formulate his plans in consultation with God rather than taking completed plans to Christ for approval. Failure to do this can result in much backtracking and a loss of face.[289]

Planning and the Prospective Missionary

Because human plans are subject to the providence of God, missionaries should always make sure that their plans are Biblical. The missionary should always ask

---

[287]J. Herbert Kane, <u>The Making of a Missionary</u> (Grand Rapids: Baker Book House, 1975), 63.

[288]Cannon, 20.

[289]Cannon, 20-21.

what Biblical reason there is for the particular activity or project under consideration. The enabling of God will only be found for those plans that are Bible-based. In addition, all planning should be done with prayer. Prayer is important for the accomplishment of any task. Every decision should be baptized in prayer. This will ensure that all planning is being done within the providence of God.[290]

As the missionary plans, he should also analyze whether he is being a "team player." Paul was aware that he could not do what had to be done without the help of others. People were strategic to him and his work. His network included people of varying personalities. Mutual dependence is necessary if the work of mission is to be fulfilled.[291]

If planning is done with these considerations in mind, the missionary has fulfilled the Pauline model in Philippians. He is now ready to work deliberately. Every missionary should know what he is doing and where he is going. There must be a strong, motivating purpose behind the missionary enterprise. If the missionary has clear goals, he can function as a true visionary, moving from place to place in the will of God.[292] The book of Philippians reveals that Paul worked hard to complete his tasks and objectives.

---

[290]Golz, 271.

[291]Golz, 271-72.

[292]Golz, 272.

All missionaries should work together to develop disciplines similar to those of Paul. Managed lives and ministries result in fewer failures and frustrations. Instead, they result in more "faithfulness, fervency, and fruitfulness, to the glory of God and the building of His church."[293]

---

[293]Golz, 272.

Chapter 8
Educational Background

"Anyone who ventures into cross-cultural missions without some kind of preparation is nuts."[294] This is the bold statement of Thomas Hale who convincingly argues that "no one should grudge the time spent" in missions preparation. He estimates that proper preparation relieves half of the stress of arrival on the field. In addition, proper preparation eliminates needless mistakes and makes one a better missionary.[295]

Exactly how much preparation is needed? The research of Nancy McCutcheon reveals that many are suggesting four years of college, including thirty hours of Bible and theology. Sixty-two and one-half percent of the mission boards who responded to her questionnaire had this basic requirement for career missionaries.[296] Obviously, most mission boards consider education a necessity. What is the purpose for this education? Are there other avenues of acceptable study outside of the college classroom? Are there dangers associated with formal education? Once again the book of Philippians (3:1-14) can provide answers.

---

[294]Thomas Hale, On Being a Missionary (Pasadena, CA: William Carey Library, 1995), 30.

[295]Hale, 30.

[296]Nancy S McCutcheon, "The Importance of Spiritual, Psychological, Academic, and Skills Preparation for Missionary Candidates" (M.A. diss., Columbia Biblical Seminary, 1993), 66.

The Purpose of Education

Thomas Hale suggests that the purpose of missionary training "is to strengthen weak areas, to improve attitudes, to provide problem-solving skills, and to hasten spiritual and emotional maturation."[297] Though education should improve the missionary's learning ability, the primary purpose is to deepen his spiritual life. The book of Philippians would tend to support this balance (3:1-3).

Doctrinal Integrity

The phrase λοιπον that begins chapter three does not necessarily carry any connotations of "in conclusion" or "farewell." The phrase could just have easily been rendered "furthermore." This introductory phrase is followed by a command to "rejoice in the Lord," that is, because they belong to the Lord. Some take this injuction to rejoice as an explanation of the undefined "same things" (3:1). Whatever these "things" are, Paul did not hesitate to write about them for they were necessary for the safety of the Philippian believers.[298]

Contextually, it appears that the phrase "same things" is looking forward to the following warnings about the enemies of the truth. Paul did not hesitate to take up this important issue, for it was the safest thing for the Philippians. No doubt Paul had already told them to be on

---

[297]Hale, 33.

[298]Ralph P. Martin, The Epistle of Paul to the Philippians (Grand Rapids: Eerdmans Publishing Company, 1987), 138-39.

guard for such false teachers. Repeated warnings were now a necessity as a safeguard.[299]

Paul's tone changed as he began to describe these false teachers. His warnings were voiced in very strong terms. Three times he used the imperative mood, βλεπετε, telling them to beware. This was obviously an earnest and tense issue with the apostle. A specific group was trying to destroy the Philippian believers, and Paul used three phrases to decribe them.

First, they were "dogs" (3:2). Dogs were regaraded by the Jews as "despised, insolent, and miserable" animals. They were considered unclean, and orthodox Jews used the term to describe despised Gentile nations. Paul, however, reversed the term and used it to describe Jewish teachers who misrepresented the truth. Ignatius described heretical teachers as "mad dogs," and that very well may be Paul's sense here. These heretical teachers were relentlessly "dogging" his steps and yelping like dogs (Psalm 59:6, 14) to impede his missionary work.[300]

Second, these false teachers were described as "evil workers" (3:2). Because these teachers had "confidence in the flesh" (3:4), there is a strong likelihood that Paul was referring to those who "worked" for salvation. All such work is evil because it undermines the merit of Christ and substitutes for it the merit of man. The Bible constantly places a strong denunciation on those who preach human merit as a means of obtaining salvation.

---

[299]Martin, 139-40.

[300]Martin, 141.

Finally, Paul referred to these false teachers as those who were "of the concision" (3:2). Paul, however, in his reference to circumcision refused to use the proper name for this rite. He instead referred to it with the word for cutting κατατομην. Their act was nothing less than a mutilation of the body, a practice condemned in the Old Testament (Leviticus 21:5).[301] In their zeal to adhere to the Old Testament, they had violated it.

Paul was very perceptive to recognize the difference between those who professed adherence to Biblical doctrine and those who actually embraced it. This is one of the most important reasons for a solid Bible education. Missionary "candidates need to know and be able to articulate their doctrinal beliefs on most major issues; they should be able to defend these beliefs with Scriptural backing."[302]

As Lunde states, "A missionary going to almost any mission field today, and surely in the future, will come into contact with one or more of these new theologies. It will become increasingly needful to recognize them and be able to deal with them."[303] Obviously, Paul perceived and understood the theological deviations of his day. This is why he was able to warn the Philippian believers of these dangers. Doctrinal confusion can come to new Christians in subtle and seemingly logical ways.

---

[301]Martin, 141.

[302]McCutcheon, 68.

[303]Joel S. Lunde, "Curriculum Proposals in Mission for the Lutheran Brethren Seminary" (D.Miss. diss., Trinity Evangelical Divinity School, 1985), 102.

Moreover, if the missionary desires to evangelize people from these doctrinal deviations, "he must establish credibility with the target people by familiarity with their religion."[304] It is presumptuous to travel to a people who have held certan heretical doctrines for years and expect a hearing when the evangelist is not well-versed in that religion. Paul was able to attack the heretical views within the Judaism of his day because he was well-versed in Judaism. The proper evangelist is one who possesses the doctrinal integrity to recognize error and refute it. He must be "able by sound doctrine both to exhort and convince the gainsayers" (Titus 1:9).

Devotional Intensity

Paul was able not only to recognize and refute "the concision;" he was also able to recognize and embrace "the circumcision who worship God" (3:3). The true name περιτομη is reserved for Christians. Thus, the word "circumcision" changes its meaning here. The thought here is not of a procedure performed on the flesh, but of a work of God performed on the heart. Even in the Old Testament economy, God had revealed that the physical rite of circumcision was inadequate.[305] True circumcision is a spiritual work in which God cuts off the sin from around man's heart.

Those who have experienced this spiritual circumcision are characterized by three qualities. First, they "worship God in Spirit." Jesus taught that worship was an intensely spiritual thing (John 4:24), and Paul echoed that sentiment here. Whatever outward forms and rituals one uses,

---

[304]Lunde, 102.

[305]Leviticus 26:41; Deuteronomy 10:16; Jeremiah 4:4.

nothing can or should detract from the spiritual quality of worship. The heart attitude of the worshipper is the primary concern (Psalm 51:17).

Another characteristic of the truly circumcised is that they "rejoice in Christ Jesus." The word καυχωμενοι is a favorite of Paul's and is used "to define two extremes of religious attitude; either proud self-confidence or humble submission to God's grace as revealed in the cross of Jesus."[306] The boasting of the believer is never in himself; this is the essence of sin (Galatians 6:13). The boasting must always be in Christ Jesus and His saving work (Galatians 6:14). The truly circumcised are characterized by a deflation of pride and an exaltation of God's grace.

Finally, those who are truly circumcised are characterized by placing "no confidence in the flesh." The true Christian has no innate tendency to secure a proper standing before God by his own effort. Paul's adversaries were characterized by a reliance on rituals and rites. Perhaps the apostle deliberately used the word "flesh" to make a connection with the rite of circumcision. True followers of God, however, are characterized by what they do "in the spirit." All self-confidence undermines the person and work of Christ, and therefore it is to be rejected.

Thus proper education not only helps the student to pinpoint doctrine and expose heresy; it also helps the student become more intimate with God through an appropriate understanding of His Word. As Lee well states, not all university students are "eligible for Christian missions, for they need spiritual qualifications as well as

---

[306]Martin, 143.

academic qualifications to be acceptable."[307]   It is not enough to possess integrity; the missionary candidate must also possess devotional intensity.

Types of Education

Paul's repudiation of "confidence in the flesh" paves the way for a full exposure of his educational experience before his conversion. He certainly was a man who was tempted to put confidence in the flesh. The recipients were given a glimpse into Paul's pre-Christian days and were able to see the educational devices in which Paul had trusted.

Certainly no other person had the credentials of the Apostle Paul. He, more than "any other man," was able to judge the issue. The Apostle Paul, who had "more" in which to glory, refuted any hypothetical debater who might point to his own résumé. Paul listed his credentials so that the reader could understand the validity of his point. He listed seven advantages in two broad categories.

Nontraditional Education

The first four items that the Apostle Paul listed were those that were his by hereditary. Every missionary is born into a certain environment by God's sovereign choice. This very environment is meant to prepare the missionary for his evangelistic activity in the future.

For example, the Apostle Paul was circumcised when he was eight days old. This proves conclusively that both

---

[307]David T. W. Lee, "A Missionary Training Program for University Students in South Korea" (D.Miss. diss., Trinity Evangelical School, 1983), 91.

of his parents conformed to the letter of the law (Leviticus 12:3). "He was no proselyte, circumcised later in life;" he was "a true-blooded Jew from the cradle, and nursed in the ancestral faith."[308] Here was an authority that very few could challenge. The one who challenged the significance of circumcision was one who had been circumcised since the eighth day of his life.

As a result, he was in every sense of the word "of the stock of Israel." He was proud to claim that he was a full-blooded Jew. Israel "was the religious name of the nation to which Paul belonged, and it meant much to a religious Jew."[309]

Within the national life of these people "who had power with God" (Genesis 32:28), Paul was of a special tribe. The tribe of Benjamin was held in high regard in spite of its smallness. This southern tribe resisted the encroachments of paganism from the north. Both the holy city and the temple were located within its boundaries. Benjamin was only one of two tribes that remained loyal to the house of David after the nation divided. Israel's first king came from this tribe, and in all likelihood the apostle was named after King Saul.[310] Thus, the apostle was not only in Judaism from birth and brought up within its religious traditions, he was also a member of one of Israel's most illustrious tribes.

---

[308]Martin, 145.

[309]Oliver B. Green, The Epistle of Paul the Apostle to the Philippians (Greenville, SC: The Gospel Hour, 1965), 83.

[310]Martin, 146.

In addition, Paul was the Hebrew son of Hebrew parents. This statement informed the readers that Paul was brought up in "the ancestral mother-tongue of his race."[311] The ability to speak the ancient languages of Hebrew and Aramaic commanded special recognition, and Paul was able to seize this advantage during his missionary career (Acts 22:2). Nancy Palmer rightly observes that "if the mission is to be more than professional competence, but a living and deep relationship with other men and women, then language mastery must be accorded a foremost place in the missionary's first term."[312] Fluency in the native tongue can hardly be overemphasized. Paul's ministry was enhanced because he possessed this ability.

In contrast, many American missionaries are monolingual and fail to recognize how much energy is needed to become fluent in a foreign tongue. Because the complexities of idiomatic sayings and humor are enormous, many missionaries have a long list of embarrassing language mistakes. These mistakes have often impeded heart-to-heart spiritual discussions.[313] Because Paul was raised in the Hebrew language, he did

---

[311]Martin, 146.

[312]Nancy N. Palmer, "Cross Cultural Training and Orientation for Missionaries with Special Reference to the North American Baptist Conference" (M.A. diss., Nazarene Theological Seminary, 1987), 56.

[313]Robert J. Campbell, "The Program of Pre-Field Orientation for Appointees with Greater Europe Mission" (D.Miss. diss., Trinity Evangelical Divinity School, 1987), 46.

not suffer the embarrassing situations that those who go to language school do.

Paul's reference to his circumcision, race, tribe, and language reveal that there is much more to missionary education than just a knowledge of Bible doctrine. Lee goes so far as to state that it is assumed that prospective missionaries "will receive a portion of their education from the secular university as a part of their missionary training program."[314] While some may shy away from such proposals not wanting any "secular influence" in the prospective missionary's education, it must be recognized that the missionary must go as a student of the culture he seeks to evangelize if he hopes to be successful in his endeavor.

This is why Lee advocates "two learning centers" in the course of missionary training. The first would be a secular university where the missionary chooses "to specialize in the development of certain major skills," while the second would be a missionary training center where the missionary concentrates on such subjects as church planting and theology of missions. While recognizing that secular education has "detrimental factors," Lee believes that there is a sense in which such education could be "pertinent."[315] If nothing else, the secular university can often supply the professional training needed for a missionary in his host culture, training that a Bible college in America could never offer.[316] It may be wise for the prospective missionary to

---

[314]Lee, iv.

[315]Lee, 71.

[316]Lee, 88.

consider prayerfully this alternative form of education if he is not fortunate enough to have it by birth, as was the Apostle Paul.

Traditional Education

After discussing what he had received through heredity, Paul turned to three privileges that were his by personal achievement (3:5-6). The Jews possessed a high devotion to the law, and Paul belonged to the strictest sect of the law's adherents; he was a Pharisee. His zeal as a Pharisee caused him to hate Christians and persecute them aggressively. No one could deny that Saul of Tarsus had been zealous in his beliefs. The memory of his zealous persecution continually haunted Paul. This was so true that Paul used the present participle of the verb διοκον, "as if the action were before his eyes at the time of writing."[317]

By human standards of legal righteousness, Paul was blameless. It is important to note Paul's carefully-worded standard. He was referring to "righteousness which is in the law." "It is only by reference to the observance of this law that his verdict can be recorded as faultless."[318] Some rabbis believed that blamelessness could be achieved through strict observation of the law. According to that standard, Paul qualified.

No one could doubt that Paul was a devoted student of the Mosaic Law. He was an honor student in the Old Testament Scriptures. This greatly helped the apostle, as he would later stand in synagogues and allege from these

---

[317]Martin, 147.

[318]Martin, 147.

same Scriptures that Jesus was the Christ. This would not have been possible if Paul had not been so proficient in the Old Testament.[319]

While there is a sense in which nothing can take the place of experience, it is equally true that there is nothing that can take the place of acquired knowledge through reading. Fortunately, much helpful and insightful literature is available today to prepare the missionary candidate for cross-cultural evangelism, and this reading material should not be minimized. "Much can be learned in anticipation of cross-cultural ministry from those who have gone before and learned it the hard way."[320]

Perhaps this is why an overwhelming number of mission agencies require reading from a prepared list of books and articles.[321] Some of the agencies surveyed actually require this to be done before orientation sessions, while others have a daily schedule for reading certain articles and chapters during the course of candidate school. Thus, while nontraditional education has much to commend it, this must be done in addition to, never in lieu of, old-fashioned book learning.

---

[319]In addition to the Old Testament Scriptures, Paul was familiar with the writings of Greek poets and philosophers. At least the literature of Epimendides was known by Paul (Acts 17:28). For further information on this topic, see Foakes Jackson and Kirsopp Lake, The Acts of the Apostles, part 1 of The Beginnings of Christianity, 5 vols. (London: Macmillan and Company, 1920), 5:246-251.

[320]Campbell, 82.

[321]Campbell, 82.

In addition, the missionary must never view this acquisition of scholastic knowledge as something that is only pertinent to missionary candidacy. Formal missionary orientation is not the end of missionary training. Every missionary should seek to continue his education process throughout his life. He should always seek to improve in areas of language, culture, and missiology.[322]

The Dangers of Education

Hale states that one of the purposes of missionary education is to make the candidate be "more adaptable and flexible."[323] Unfortunately, education often has a tendency to make one harsh and austere (1 Corinthians 8:1). As Lush states, however, "a choice must be made related to new patterns." The missionary must unlearn some things before learning something different, "and unlearning is more difficult than learning for the first time."[324] Nevertheless, this is what the Apostle Paul had to do. He had to radically reassess his spiritual life.

Whatever was gain to Paul, he counted it as loss for Christ (3:7). The words "for Christ" explain the motive and the reason for this dramatic change. "Because of all that Christ had become to him Paul was willing to collect

---

[322]Palmer, 62.

[323]Hale, 33.

[324]Ron Lush, "Committed to Serve, Prepared to Lead: A Leadership Development Curriculum for International and Cross-Cultural Christian Ministry Leadership" (D. Min. diss., Western Seminary, 1999), 55-56.

all his former privileges, described in verses 5-6, to put them, as it were, in one parcel, and write that off as lost."[325] The strengths of the Apostle Paul were not viewed with mere indifference; they were rejected as liabilities. The contrast between "gain" and "loss" was a common teaching tool in Jewish thought,[326] and Paul used that method here.

The things that were gain to the apostle, he "counted" as loss. The verb tense is perfect, denoting a completed event with abiding results. At his conversion Paul instantaneously and consciously decided to count his personal résumé as a detriment. This included not only the advantages listed in the previous verses, but "all things" (3:8). Anything that might be viewed as meritorious was rejected. "Whatever may be regarded as a prop to support the person who hankers after something to boast about and is blind to the fact that he or she can live only by the grace of God, or as a virtue which he would call his own, is counted loss and rubbish."[327]

Indeed, even after conversion the Christian is tempted to rely on things other than Christ. Thus, Paul changed the verb tense from perfect to present tense. The preeminent role of the Christian life is "the knowledge of Christ Jesus." Everything else must be considered subordinate to this. The fellowship with Christ that was initiated the day of Paul's conversion had to be cultivated on a daily basis.

---

[325]Martin, 148.

[326]For example, Matthew 16:26; Mark 8:36.

[327]Martin, 149.

This intimate relationship "was not secured without a price."[328] Paul had to forfeit his "gains" and surrender his pride. The aorist tense suggests that this took place on a definite occasion: Paul's conversion on the road to Damascus. Through this transformation of perspective Paul was able to dismiss his former credentials as "dung." The term σκυβαλα was used of both human waste and unwanted food consigned to the rubbish heap. Some have sought to connect the term with the "dogs" mentioned in verse two. The word conveyed both distaste and disgrace and conveyed to the reader "how completely the apostle [had] turned from his pre-converted ways."[329] God estimates religious observances that stress human merit with such contemptuous terms. It therefore must be cast aside and viewed with contempt.

All must be counted loss to gain Christ. The personal appropriation of Jesus must be considered everything. The goal of the Christian life is to be "found in him" (3:9). To be in Christ means that a person will not claim his "own righteousness," but rather the righteousness "which is through the faith of Christ." A person must possess a righteousness that has been imputed by God. No human effort on the basis of the law will do; men need "the righteousness which is of God." The phrase looks back to Isaiah 54:17 where God is revealed to be "the sole author of the saving righteousness imparted to sinful men."[330] The medium through which this righteousness reaches man is "faith," specifically faith in Christ.

---

[328]Martin, 150.

[329]Martin, 150.

[330]Martin, 151.

God's righteousness that is received by faith in Christ makes it possible for the believer to know Christ (3:10). Pentecost comments that this knowledge of Christ is "an appetite for the person of Christ."[331] Paul wanted to know Christ in a personal, intimate way. This became the consuming passion of his life.

In addition, Paul wanted to know the resurrection power that is available to every Christian. The same power that brought Jesus Christ forth from the tomb is available to the believer so that he might "conquer sin daily and live a life of daily holiness and dedication."[332] The only reason that a Christian can live an effective powerful life is because Christ lives in him (Galatians 2:20).

This power helps the Christian experience the fellowship of Christ's sufferings. When Paul wrote to the Philippians, he was imprisoned and in danger of death. This imprisonment and its accompanying difficulties were part of Paul's sufferings. These sufferings, however, were not simply personal afflictions. They were understood in a much deeper sense to be a part of the sufferings of Christ. The apostle's suffering, then, was not a sign of God's displeasure with him. On the contrary, this

---

[331]J. Dwight Pentecost, The Joy of Living (Grand Rapids: Zondervan Publishing House, 1973), 138.

[332]Oliver B. Greene, The Epistle of Paul the Apostle to the Philippians (Greenville, SC: The Gospel Hour, 1965), 90.

suffering was a privilege. It was suffering for the sake of Christ.[333]

In addition, this power helps a Christian conform to Christ's death. This conformity is best understood in light of Romans 6, which Martin says reveals "the death and resurrection of Christ [as] representative acts in which His people share."[334] Because the believer is "in Christ," he is able to die to the old nature and rise to a new spiritual standard of living.

In this way the apostle is able to "attain unto the resurrection of the dead" (3:11). Paul's reference here is not to the resurrection of the body. Paul stood in no doubt of that resurrection. A cursory reading of 1 Corinthians 15 will prove this to be true. The resurrection under discussion, then, is a completely different resurrection, for the resurrection of the body does not depend upon one's service. Paul wanted to realize in his daily walk "what it is to have been resurrected with Christ."[335]

This was the purpose for which Christ Jesus called Paul (3:12), and Paul wanted to fulfill that purpose. The apostle wanted to make as his own possession the purpose for which Christ apprehended him. He frankly confessed, however, that he had not attained this goal. He denied "any sense of final perfection as a present experience." He acknowledges that the work of sanctification is

---

[333]Peter T. O'Brien. "The Fellowship Theme in Philippians," Reformed Theological Review 37, no. 1 (1978), 12-13.

[334]Martin, 152-53.

[335]Pentecost, 141.

progressive, that the work of salvation has begun, but it is not final. "Final perfection cannot be expected in this life and there will always be room for progress while the church is God's pilgrim people.[336] This progression is the consuming drive of the Christian experience.

This is what the Christian is to "follow after." The verb διωκω is a hunting word. It is a strong word for "an earnest and active endeavor."[337] Paul wanted to pursue and overtake this goal. He pressed on because he realized he was not yet perfect. The fact that ultimate perfection is not attainable in this life did not prohibit Paul from keeping perfection as his goal. On the contrary, he strained with every fiber of his being to persue the goal before him.

Thus, there is a significant balance in the life of the Apostle Paul. "There is no complacency which cuts the nerve of progress or stifles the hope of final perfection; and no sinful contentment with his own present position."[338] Paul's ambition was to forget what was behind, whether success or failure, and press on. The temptation was always present to have confidence in the flesh. Such confidence, however, would impede the Apostle's progress. This temptation was avoided by a constant and deliberate forgetting.

Remembering in the Biblical sense carries the connotation of recalling a past act into the present so that the past act is potently present (I Kings 17:18). Paul said

---

[336]Martin, 154-55.

[337]Martin, 155.

[338]Martin, 155.

that he must forget his past in this sense. He should not allow his past to have any influence upon his spiritual outlook or conduct.[339]

Instead he had to look to the future. Like a runner, the apostle had to make every effort to press forward. He had to finish the race and obtain the prize (3:14). Paul did not define this "prize," but the reader is given some clues in the phrase "of the high calling." The words do not denote the content of the prize. Instead, they state "that God's call has come to him in order that he might enter for and attain the prize."[340]   The call had been given on the Damascus Road, and Paul had responded to it. It had been given to him by Jesus Christ and led the apostle to God. It, therefore, seems best to believe that the "prize" was God Himself.   Any notion of personal merit must be excluded because God called and enabled him by divine grace to receive the prize.

Education and the Prospective Missionary

Thus, while the missionary understands that there is a purpose to the various types of education, he must never place his confidence in these credentials. It is true that a missionary can be under-trained, but it is equally true, as in the case of Paul, that a missionary can be over-trained. If the missionary is not careful, his advanced degrees may cause him to be useless on the mission field. Often the highly educated missionary can feel that certain jobs are beneath him.[341]

---

[339]Martin, 156.

[340]Martin, 157.

[341]Hale, 31.

It is imperative that the missionary constantly check his motives. Does he intend his education to be a "safety net" in case he decides to go home? Does his pursuit of advanced degrees unnecessarily delay his departure to the field? "The danger is very great" that the missionary "will lose the vision. Procrastination equals disobedience."[342]

Education can also lead the missionary to rely on professional qualifications rather than the Spirit of God. Every missionary must guard against "confidence in the flesh," and advanced education can make this all the more difficult. When the missionary begins to rely on skill rather than the Spirit, he is in trouble. God's enabling must be the missionary's consuming desire. According to Paul, the knowledge of Christ makes all other attainments appear as "dung." "Our qualifications are not what produce the fruit that lasts; only the Holy Spirit working through us can do that."[343]

---

[342]Hale, 32.

[343]Hale, 32.

Chapter 9
Philosophy of Separation

Fred Moritz, executive director of Baptist World Mission, firmly believes that "separation complements evangelism."[344] He convincingly argues that evangelism and separation are not at odds. To the contrary, Scripture blends separation[345] and evangelism together as companion philosophies (2 Corinthians 5:17-7:1). "The forced division between the strategies of evangelism and separatism is an unnatural dichotomy when evaluated by biblical standards."[346]

The book of Philippians (3:15-21) would tend to support Moritz's conclusions. Evangelism and separation are joined together in Scripture and cannot be separated. Separation aids evangelism. Sadly, many missionaries have forsaken separation in order to emphasize evangelism. Such missionary activity ignores the Biblical teaching about separation, and "it distorts, weakens, and

---

[344]Fred Moritz, Be Ye Holy (Greenville, SC: Bob Jones University Press, 1994), 4.

[345]For a complete Biblical treatment of the doctrine of separation, see Douglas R. McLachlan, Reclaiming Authentic Fundamentalism (Independence, MO: American Association of Christian Schools), 114-42. McLachlan presents a Scriptural view of personal, ecclesiastical, and familial separation.

[346]Moritz, 48.

compromises the gospel message in evangelism."[347] Indeed, "the great threat of heresy is countered by a strong re-statement of the Gospel."[348]

The Prerequisite to Separation

Paul's ongoing discussion about Christian perfectionism was obviously set in a context of controversy. In the Philippian church there were apparently those who thought differently from the Apostle Paul (3:15). Paul's choice of the word φρονωμεν reveals that this was more than an intellectual difference. These divergent thought processes "affected the conduct of those whom Paul has in mind."[349] Some in Philippi were teaching that final and complete perfection was possible in this life.

Paul responded to this theological disagreement with a twofold answer. He first insisted "on a true evaluation of perfection in terms of a maturity which ever seeks a fuller maturity."[350] In other words, true maturity does not assume a close-minded position that is opposed to Biblical argument. If these opponents were truly mature as they professed, they would have been open to discussion.

---

[347]Moritz, 64.

[348]Patrick Rogers, "Hopeful in Spite of Chains," <u>Biblical Theology Bulletin</u> 12, no. 3 (1982), 79.

[349]Ralph P. Martin, <u>The Epistle of Paul to the Philippians</u> (Grand Rapids: Eerdmans Publishing Company, 1987), 158.

[350]Martin, 158.

Second, Paul discounted their claim of absolute perfection by appealing to God. Paul was confident that he had spoken the truth, and thus he appealed for divine illumination, knowing that "God is able to correct the behavior of those who [did] not share his conviction."[351]

The implication of the apostle was that all Christians should have a desire to know the truth. God's revelation is always given to those who have a desire to know the truth (3:16). Thus, the people of God should be teachable and open-minded. Christians should guide their lives according to the truth that they have received and should desire even greater light so that they might understand the Word of God more perfectly.

The apostle himself lived in this manner, and his example is to be followed (3:17). A Christian may follow all the precepts and maxims of the Christian life and still not conform to the spirit of Christian living. The Christian life is the worship of God "in spirit and in truth" (John 4:24). It is the life of the Lord Jesus Christ fleshed out in His followers. Even the command given here to follow the Apostle Paul should be understood in the light of 1 Corinthians 11:1. We follow Paul because Paul followed Christ.

The example of Paul, as mentioned earlier in Philippians 3, is an abandonment of confidence in the flesh. It is a renunciation of all self-righteousness. This attitude is a prerequisite to separation. The separatist must never implement his axioms of separation in order to gloat in his own self-righteousness. The missionary must always practice the principle of separation, not because he desires to look better than others, but because he has an

---

[351]Moritz, 64.

overwhelming love for the truth that supersedes all other relationships.

"In the flesh we can stress purity without love."[352] Schaeffer may be right when he states that the separatist movement has often been characterized by "a hardness, a lack of love."[353] Moritz agrees. "Paul unequivocally speaks the truth in the following verses, but he does so with love for his readers and a desire that they lead Spirit-filled lives."[354] The separatist must have a genuine concern for the person from whom he separates. Paul's separation took place with tears[355] rather than flags and banners. The separatist movement is rooted in love: love for God, love for God's truth, and even love for those from whom he must separate. This is an important and necessary prerequisite to separation.

The Practice of Separation

Once the heart attitude of the separatist is correct, he is prepared to engage in the act of separation. Many professing Christians live in such a way that the name of Christ is disgraced and the hearts of other believers are pained. Even though these people are professing believers, they are "enemies of the cross of Christ" (3:18).

---

[352]Francis A. Schaeffer, The Great Evangelical Disaster (Westchester, IL: Crossway Books, 1984), 70.

[353]Schaeffer, 74-75.

[354]Moritz, 93.

[355]Moritz, 96.

When human merit is stressed as a means of obtaining salvation, the all-sufficient sacrifice of Christ is subverted and undermined. Those who embrace such theology reveal that their "end is destruction" (3:19). They have cut themselves off "from the only hope of salvation in Christ alone."[356] There is no other prospect for such men than the lake of fire that awaits all unsaved humanity.

This is true because their "God is their belly." The highest goal of these false theologians is the satisfaction and elevation of self. By making themselves the source of righteousness, the ones in error are guided by what satisfies and pleases them rather than what pleases God.[357]

In so doing, the false teacher reveals that his glory is actually shame. Paul may have been referring to their reliance upon the physical act of circumcision in which they prided themselves. If this was true, the shame would be "the nakedness of the human body required for the rite to be performed."[358] He said they "mind earthly things" because their confidence was placed in rites and rituals rather than the spiritual work that Christ alone can do in the heart.

When doctrinal heresy is being propagated, the missionary must "mark" those who are doing it. The word σκοπειτε means to "watch" and "contemplate." The noun form was used of a watchman, and then of a mark on

---

[356]Martin, 161.

[357]J. Dwight Pentecost, <u>The Joy of Living</u> (Grand Rapids: Zondervan Publishing House, 1973), 157.

[358]Martin, 161.

which to fix the eye.[359]   Kittel states that the word means "to look at critically" and was used of a judge, philosopher, or historian. The word was also used of "one who in the theater [inspected] the faces of spectators with reference to their callings." Thus, the word means "to consider something critically and then to hold something before one as a model on the basis of this inspection."[360] "The practice of truth requires that a line be drawn between those who hold to the historic view of Scripture" and those who hold to the "new weaker one."[361]   Moritz rightly affirms that fundamentalists "assert that separation cannot be repudiated as a strategy because it is founded in Biblical theology and is plainly commanded by Scripture."[362]

When the cardinal truths of the Bible are abandoned, the missionary must separate from those who have erred. This separation must be done with love, but it must be done. "Scripture commands that we must do more than just talk about the purity of the visible church; we must actually practice it, even when it is costly."[363]   This is the process that the missionary must initiate and complete.

---

[359]W.E. Vine, Vine's Expository Dictionary of New Testament Words (McLean, VA: MacDonald Publishing Company, n.d.), 724-25.

[360]G. Kittel and G. Friedrich, eds., Theological Dictionary of the New Testament, trans. G. W. Bromiley, no. 7 (Grand Rapids: Eerdmans Publishing Company, 1964-68), 414-15.

[361]Schaeffer, 89-90.

[362]Moritz, 2.

[363]Schaeffer, 70

A Motivation for Separation

Those who "mind earthly things" are set in direct contrast to those who have a citizenship in heaven (3:20). The word "our" is placed at the beginning of the sentence structure for emphasis. It is our citizenship that is in heaven, not those who have abandoned the Bible's doctrine of grace. In spite of the fact that he lives here on earth, the Christian has a home in heaven.[366]

Thus, the Philippian believers actually had two citizenships. As Roman subjects, they were citizens of Rome, in spite of its distance from Philippi. Similarly, they were citizens of heaven in spite of its tremendous distance from Philippi. "As servants of another king, one called Jesus, they are citizens of that capital city, where the King of kings has his domicile, and whose advent to establish his reign on this earth and rescue his people is awaited."[367]

From his capital city of heaven, the Christian awaits his "Savior." In Greek religion the gods were viewed as "saviors," and in Caesar worship the emperor was so named. In 48 BC the people of Ephesus declared Julius Caesar to be the universal savior of mankind. From that time forward, the ruling Caesar bore this title. In a similar way, the Christian must view the Lord Jesus Christ as the Savior who "will bring the final deliverance from all the trials and persecutions of a hostile and alien world." Christ will vindicate His people and deliver them from oppression.[368]

---

[366]Martin, 162-63.

[367]Martin, 163.

[368]Martin, 163-64.

The picture goes back to Isaiah 35:4 and other similar Old Testament passages where God comes to aid His afflicted people. The Christian is looking for this. While those who have polluted the Gospel's teaching of grace will be destroyed, those who have accepted God's grace will be saved.

Thus, while the glory of the false teachers will be turned into shame because they mind earthly things, the Christian will find himself in heaven where his vile body will be glorified (3:21). The word ταπεινωσεως refers to that which is of low estate. The earthly human body is characterized this way because it belongs to a state of humiliation through sin. Weakness and frailty characterize this body. One day, however, it will be changed to be like the glorious body of our Lord (1 Corinthians 15:42-51). The glorified body of the risen Lord is a prototype of the believer's glorified body. The believer's body will be fashioned like the Lord's body. There will be a sharing of nature of the exalted body.[369]

This sharing is possible because God is able "to subdue all things unto himself" (3:21). "Paul is making it clear that the power required to change the bodies of believers is adequately provided for in the greater assurance that He is able to subject not only the intractable elements in the believer's makeup, but everything, the entire universe, under his control."[370]

The motivation then for separation is that this world is not our final place of residence. In a very real sense the Christian is a resident alien who is dwelling temporarily in

---

[369]Martin, 165-66.

[370]Martin, 166.

a foreign country. Why should the Christian then allow the relationships and ties of this foreign country to dominate his actions and attitudes? A proper separation from the things of this world is possible when the missionary remembers that this world is not his place of permanent residence. All decisions must be made in light of his true citizenship.

When the Scriptures are being destroyed, the missionary must have the courage to mark those who are doing so. Do our current missionary candidates have the courage to do this? Can they draw the line and do so publicly? "If we do not have the courage, we will cut the ground out from under the feet of our children, and we will destroy any hope of being the redeeming salt and light of our dying generation."[371]

Schaeffer rightly recognizes that this "will not be easy, and for many it will be costly. It certainly will not be popular."[372] The missionary must recognize, however, that he is not being sent to conform to the popular theological notions of the day. He is being sent as an ambassador who represents Christ, and he must one day return to that King and give an account of what he did in an alien and hostile land. A true remembrance of this future day should provide all the motivation he needs to live a separated life.

Separation and the Prospective Missionary

Moritz has done all missionaries a service by stressing the balance of separation and evangelism. They are

---

[371]Schaeffer, 67.

[372]Schaeffer, 67.

171

compatible strategies. Fundamentalists sometimes over-emphasize separation to the neglect of evangelism, while evangelicals often stress the importance of evangelism to the neglect of separation. All Biblical separatists need to remember that "separation is not an end in itself, but a biblical strategy to be employed in tandem with evangelism."[373] When separation is emphasized to the neglect of missions, the purpose and effect of separation is stymied.

---

[373]Moritz, 65.

Chapter 10
Financial Participation

Money is a sensitive subject. Many pastors shy away from preaching on finances altogether. Others temper Biblical admonitions with apologies. The United States culture is so plagued with materialism that when the American pastor addresses the subject of giving, he recognizes that he is asking many to part with their deity.

If the work of missions is to be done, however, money is required. "If finances were unnecessary, many of God's people would lose their opportunity to invest in world evangelization."[374] To eradicate any discussion of financial stewardship from one's theology of missions is to rob the believer of the blessing that could be his.

Mission work requires money. The expense to send a missionary to the field and keep him there can be astronomical. If people are willing to go, however, churches should be willing to shoulder the financial responsibility of sending missionaries to and maintaining missionaries in their God-appointed areas. Indeed, God is so involved in the financial support of missions that He calls missionary giving a "grace" (2 Corinthians 8:1). Giving is "a privilege extended to us by God."[375] Since God is so involved with missionary giving, one should expect to find within the pages of Philippians principles for financial participation in missions (4:1-23).

---

[374]Melbourne E. Cuthbert, ed., Managing Missions in the Local Church (Cherry Hill, NJ: Association of Baptists for World Evangelism, 1987), 125.

[375]Cuthbert, 125.

The Prerequisites for Financial Participation

While some have taken the exhortation to "stand fast in the Lord" (4:1) as rounding off the previous section of the Philippian correspondence, the phrase may be "a solemn and formal introduction to what follows."[376] Paul possessed a consuming desire to see the Philippian believers again. They were his "joy and crown." The word στεφανος was used to denote a festive garland that was awarded to the winner of an athletic contest. The Philippian believers were Paul's reward and proof that his labor had not been in vain.[377] This being the case, the church at Philippi was asked to "stand fast in the Lord." They were asked to possess certain inner qualities of the Christian life. These qualities serve as important prerequisites to Paul's admonitions about missionary giving.

Love

The first of these prerequisites is love. Eudoias and Syntyche were ladies in the Philippian church who quarreled with each other in spite of the fact that they "labored with" Paul "in the gospel" (4:3). Perhaps they assisted Paul with material help as other ladies had done (Acts 16:15, 40). Paul regretted that they were at odds with one another, and he admonished them to "be of the same mind in the Lord" (4:2). Clearly, then, their disagreement was serious; it had "ecclesiastical repercussions."[378]

---

[376]Ralph P. Martin, The Epistle of Paul to the Philippians (Grand Rapids: Eerdmans Publishing Company, 1987), 167.

[377]Martin, 167.

[378]Martin, 168.

As a result of their conflicts, Paul had to enlist the help of another member in the church to assist with the reconciliation of these two women. If the reader assumes that the phrase συζυγεγνησιε refers to a proper name, one can conclude that Paul intended a pun similar to that used in reference to Onesimus (Philemon 11). Syzygus was appropriately named, for he was a true yoke-fellow. He certainly would be able to bring together these estranged women. Others, including Clement, would assist Syzygus in this endeavor. Clearly Paul desired love to exist in the Philippian church, for giving is not done rightly if it is not administered from a heart of love (1 Corinthians 13:3).

Joy

In addition to manifesting love, the Philippian church was supposed to manifest joy (4:4). This was possible because the Philippian believers were "in the Lord." Paul's command to rejoice throws them back on the Lord. Through dependence in Him, they could rejoice despite their outward circumstances.

This dependency upon Christ for the capacity to rejoice is essential in light of the fact that the believer is commanded to be gracious to "all men" (4:5). Graciousness is to be shown, not only among one's close inner circle of Christian friends, but to one's relations in the outside world. The Christian should yield when he is under trial and refuse to retaliate when he is attacked. Though these actions are impossible to the natural man, the Christian who possesses the joy of the Lord will be able to do it. Such graciousness is important in light of the fact that the Lord's return is at hand.

Thus, joy is another imperative in the life of one who would be a financial participant in world evangelism.

175

Paul told that Corinthian church that God loves "a cheerful giver" (2 Corinthians 9:7). "Proper giving is joyful giving."[379]

Peace

Unfortunately, many Christians cannot give joyfully because they are filled with anxiety over finances. Anxiety, however, betrays a lack of trust in the providential care of God. This sinful anxiety can be alleviated through prayer. "We may be freed from all fretful care and feverish anxiety because we may refer all our distresses and problems to God in prayer."[380] Such prayers should be filled "with thanksgiving." By concentrating on the goodness and provision of God, anxiety over potential distress will be alleviated.

When the believer engages in prayer, the peace of God is given (4:7).[381] The genitive "of God" denotes origin; it is the peace that God alone can give. This divine peace surpasses human understanding because it is able to protect the mind under the most trying circumstances. "The Philippians, living in a garrison town, would [have been] familiar with the sight of the Roman sentry, maintaining his watch."[382] God's peace is able to protect the heart and mind of the believer, allowing him to "keep" his mind when he should be losing it.

---

[379]Don Sisk, Joyful Giving (Milford, OH: John the Baptist Printing Ministry, 1992), 8.

[380]Martin, 171.

[381]See Isaiah 26:3.

This tremendous gift of peace is available "through Christ Jesus," that is, by one's "obedience to him and submission to his authority."[383] Obedience and submission are accomplished by thinking on the proper things (4:8). The believer must reflect upon certain things and allow these things to shape his conduct. An ethical list follows, but rather than prolong the list of desirable qualities, Paul summed up all the virtues that he might have listed with the words "if there be any virtue, and if there be any praise." The word "virtue" can signify "both excellence in any sphere of activity and the prestige which such excellence acquires." The word "praise" refers to any quality that might "call down the approval of God."[384] Thinking on these types of activities will help keep the believer in the peace of God.

Nothing proves this true more than the life of the Apostle Paul himself. Paul had exemplified the traits he commanded. The Philippian believers knew this to be true, for they had seen these character traits in the apostle (4:9). This was an incentive for the Philippian believers to develop these qualities in themselves, for they had witnessed the residual peace in the life of Paul. When a person does the things outlined in this passage, the God of peace will be with him, and the Apostle Paul's life proved this to be true.

Paul had learned the contentment of God's peace. Paul was able to rejoice when the Philippians illustrated their generosity to him (4:10). The arrival of their financial assistance prompted the apostle to rejoice in the Lord. The Philippian believers had thought of Paul once again. The term ανεθαλετε was borrowed from the horticulture

---

[383]Martin, 173.

[384]Martin, 174.

practice of Paul's time. It denoted "plants and flowers blooming again."[385] The concern of the Philippians had revived. This is not to say that the Philippians had not been concerned for Paul. Indeed, they had been, but they lacked an opportunity to manifest that concern. Paul did not attach blame, for circumstances were beyond their control.

Paul stated clearly that he was not disappointed in them. This was true because Paul "had learned the secret of deep peace based on detachment from his outward circumstances."[386] In whatever conditions of life Paul found himself, he was able to detach himself from anxious care about the features of life (4:11).

Paul explained this detachment by stating that he knew how to be abased and how to abound. He knew how to be full and to be hungry. He knew how to abound and how to suffer need (4:12). Indeed, it is an impressive testimony, but "his self-sufficiency and equanimity in meeting all life's demands [had] not come through a mechanical self-discipline or fixed resolution such as the stoic practiced."[387] It was "through Christ" (4:13) that Paul was able to do these things. Paul insisted that the believer could find the adequate strength to meet every possible situation of life because of his vital union with the Savior.

This great contentment in Paul's life did not negate his appreciation for the Philippian believers' benevolence. "They had identified themselves with the apostle in

---

[385]Martin, 177.

[386]Martin, 177.

[387]Martin, 179.

partnership on behalf of the work of the gospel."[388] Paul commended the entire congregation. "It [was] the church that entered into partnership in giving and receiving."[389] In so doing, they participated in Paul's present affliction.

Though this act of Christian benevolence caused Paul to rejoice, it did not add to his contentment. Paul had determined to be content even when abased, hungry, and needy. This type of contentment, along with love and joy, was what Paul desired for the Philippian believers. According to Philippians, love, joy, and peace are important prerequisites to one's financial participation in missions.

The Prospect of Financial Participation

Paul praised the Philippian church for their missionary giving and referred to their contributions as "giving and receiving" (4:15).   The Greek phrase, δοσεως και λημψεως, refers to "a double transaction."[390] This was a standard way of referring to credits and debits, expressing the two sides of the ledger.[391] In other words, when the Philippians "communicated" with Paul, their expenditure resulted in some tangible benefit. Because they gave, they received something in return. Indeed, the phrase "as concerning," εις λογον, may also be translated "to the

---

[388]Martin, 180.

[389]Peter T. O'Brien, "The Fellowship Theme in Philippians," Reformed Theological Review 37, no.1 (1978), 15.

[390]Martin, 181.

[391]Gregory J. Mazak, "The Peace of the Christian Life," Biblical Viewpoint 26, no.1, (1992), 4.

account of."[392] Though the Philippians may have forfeited their finances, the transaction was not entirely negative. Something was received, and a deposit was made in their account.

To help the reader understand the nature of this tangible blessing, Paul referred to the time of their gift. This time of "giving and receiving" took place "in the beginning of the gospel," when Paul "departed from Macedonia" (4:15). The reference was to Paul's second missionary journey when he first proclaimed the Gospel in Macedonia (Acts 17:1-5). "When he left Macedonia (the location of Philippi) to travel south to Achaia (where Corinth was located),"[393] the Philippian church was the only local assembly that supported him. His first major stop after leaving Philippi was Thessalonica, one hundred miles away. Here, even before he entered Achaia, the Philippian believers sent "once and again" (4:16) to Paul's need.

This "necessity" evidently referred to the troubles Paul had experienced in Thessalonica. When Luke told of Paul's missionary activity in Thessalonica, he reported "no vivid conversion stories" but contented himself "with a general summary of Paul's evangelism"[394] The preaching of the apostle had been effective. Jews, Gentile adherents of the synagogue, and certain leading women had all been converted to the faith. The latter were "wives of

---

[392]Mazak, 47.

[393]Mazak, 47.

[394]I. Howard Marshall, The Acts of the Apostles (Grand Rapids: Eerdmans Publishing Company, 1980), 277.

leading men."[395] Kent suggests that it was the conversion of these women that triggered the animosity of the Jewish authorities. "Perhaps they resented the loss of financial support from the wealthy women who had been converted to Christ."[396] Whatever the case, the threat of the authorities forced the Christians to send Paul and Silas away secretly at night, leaving the small church that they had just planted behind. The Philippians, hearing about the troubles in Thessalonica, responded with a gift that enabled Paul to continue his missionary endeavors.

In addition, the Philippian church was the "only" church to support Paul at this time (4:15). Had it not been for the Philippian church, humanly speaking there would have not been a church at Thessalonica, or any epistles to the church at Thessalonica. "If he could not go back to Thessalonica in person, he could write the church a letter."[397] In addition, there would have been no church at Corinth, or any epistles to the church at Corinth. Without financial support from Philippi, there would have been no church at Ephesus and no subsequent epistle to the church there. In other words, three churches were planted and five books of the Bible were made possible by the missionary giving of the church at Philippi.

When a local church chooses to invest money in the missionary enterprise, the prospects are limitless. The

---

[395]William Neil, <u>Acts</u> (Grand Rapids: Eerdmans Publishing Company, 1973), 187.

[396]Homer A. Kent, <u>Jerusalem to Rome</u> (Grand Rapids: Baker Book House, 1972), 137.

[397]John Phillips, <u>Exploring Acts</u> (Neptune, NJ: Loizeaux Brothers, 1986), 341.

believer has no idea how God will take his money and produce churches in pagan cultures. Missionary giving causes the Word of God to progress in ways never before imagined. Thus the Philippian believers received much more than they gave. They received the joy of seeing churches planted and God's Word advanced. This was the result of their financial participation in missions.

The Procedure of Financial Participation

In Paul's statement on missionary giving to the church at Philippi, an underlying principle exists. Christian giving should be done through the auspices of a local New Testament church. Paul makes it clear that "no church" communicated gifts with him (4:15). In other words, Paul sought his missionary support from churches. When Paul instituted assistance for the poor saints in Jerusalem, he did so through the agency of local churches. The people at Corinth were told to give on the first day of the week (1 Corinthians 16:1-2). Where would they be on the first day of the week? They would be in church. Their financial gifts were to be laid by "in store." Many Christian writers have argued that there is not a New Testament storehouse. Paul would beg to differ. Systematic giving was to be done through the local church. Instructions for missionary giving were distributed to "the churches of Galatia." Paul's second letter to Corinth also described giving "as the grace of God bestowed on the churches of Macedonia" (2 Corinthians 8:1). Financial participation in missions was to be done through the local church.

To Protect Anonymity

Jesus told His disciples that when they gave, their right hand was not to know what their left hand had done (Matthew 6:1-4). He said that giving should be done in secret. The Christian should not "blow his own horn." Giving, as much as is humanly possible, should be done anonymously. When this principle is violated, favoritism is often shown. As Proverbs states, "A man's gift maketh room for him, and bringeth him before great men" (Proverbs 18:16). Whether it is one's motive or not, when a gift is given personally to another man, the potential for favoritism is there.

When a man gives a personal gift to another man, the receiver is indebted to the giver. Many churches are blessed with benevolent people. Businessmen often employ other believers in the congregation. When Christians are hurting financially, those who are capable may help with groceries and the like. The residual problem of such activity, however, is that those who were helped feel indebted to those who were benevolent. When gifts are given individually, rather than institutionally, the temptation to favoritism exists.

When Paul went to help the poor in Jerusalem, he did not encourage people to personally take money and give it to the poor. Instead, he encouraged churches to set up funds. Believers were to give to the church, and the church would give it to the poor people. In this way, no one who had received money knew who gave the money. "Right hands" did not know what "left hands" were doing. Trumpets were not sounded. No one felt obligated to any certain individual. The only thing to which people were indebted was the church of Jesus Christ.

This is not to say that Christians should never directly help people who need it. Systematic giving, however, should go through the storehouse. This procedure protects the dignity of the poor and the secrecy of the donor. Giving should be done through the church storehouse in order to protect anonymity.

To Protect Continuity

Missionary projects were not the only funds that the Apostle Paul instituted through churches. His personal missionary support was garnered through churches as well, not through individuals. The Apostle Paul indicated that he did not receive missionary support from individuals. Paul referred to his missionary support as coming through churches (4:15).

When a missionary is funded through a local church, rather than an individual, there will be continuity to the Lord's work. For example, when a missionary appointee travels to a local church and presents his work, there may be an elderly lady in the church who is financially blessed. She may be impressed with the young missionary and volunteer to support him personally for two hundred dollars per month. This is a significant percentage of the appointee's support level, and he immediately assumes that this generous suggestion is of the Lord. He graciously accepts this elderly lady's proposal. His support comes in more rapidly by taking personal support than it would have if he had limited himself to church support alone. He reaches the field quickly, only to discover during his first term that the elderly lady who supports him for two hundred dollars a month now has Alzheimer's disease and is in a nursing home. Her sister has been given power of attorney. The missionary now finds his support level lessened by two hundred dollars per month. A few months later, another donor dies. A year later a rich man who invested in the missionary suffers a severe financial setback. The missionary now discovers that he must return from the field to raise additional support. The work on the mission field is interrupted. The continuity of the

Lord's work has been broken, all because giving was not done through a local church. All of this could have been avoided if the missionary would have received his financial support through a local church.

To Solidify Commitment

The book of Acts states the requirements for church membership (Acts 2:41-42). These verses are not talking about the universal church, as the order of the verses reveals. People received the Word. They were baptized. They were added unto the church. If this were talking about the universal church, the order would be salvation, admission to the church, and then baptism. Baptism in water has nothing to do with membership in the universal church. A person is placed in the body of Christ at the moment of conversion whether he has been baptized or not. Baptism is, however, a prerequisite to local church membership. Baptism is the believer's public identification with the Lord Jesus Christ, and a Christian cannot be identified with a local church until he has first made his faith in Christ public through the ordinance of baptism. Therefore, one should not be allowed to become a church member before he is a saved and Scripturally baptized individual. Only after he is saved and baptized can he be added unto the church. God's sovereign order is salvation, baptism, and church membership.

How, then, is one added to the local church? He is added based on his creed and conduct. Acts 2:42 states that church members are those who continue steadfastly in apostolic doctrine. By reading the New Testament, one discovers the teaching of the apostles. The apostles, under the inspiration of the Holy Spirit, taught the church what to believe and how to behave. In other words, when one joins a church, he is promising to that local assembly that

185

he will believe certain things and behave in a certain way. Church membership, then, is a look to the past and a look to the future. As far as the past is concerned, the new member testifies that he has been saved and scripturally baptized. As far as the future is concerned, he states that he will continue to believe certain things and behave in a certain way. He will continue in apostolic teaching.

These two elements of apostolic doctrine (what to believe and how to behave) are commonly referred to as the "doctrinal statement" and "church covenant" of a local assembly. The church's doctrinal statement refers to creeds and beliefs. The church's covenant refers to conduct and behavior.

Moreover, the covenant of most churches contains something about giving. Usually the church covenant contains a provision about church members supporting the church with prayers, presence, and financial substance. Church members covenant with one another to give to the local assembly.

When a person joins a church, then, he promises to believe certain things and behave in a certain way, and part of how he promises to behave is to contribute to the local church. If, therefore, a person is a member of a local church, and he is not contributing to the assembly, more than likely he is breaking a covenant. Each member has a responsibility and commitment to the church with which he is affiliated, and giving solidifies that commitment.

To Recognize Authority

God considers Christian giving so important that He put an authority over it. God ordained certain men to "serve tables" (Acts 6:3-4). Although these men were not

186

specifically called "deacons," cognate words do occur in the chapter three times (Acts 6:1, 2, and 4). "Inasmuch as the epistles indicate the existence of officers called deacons who appear to be secondary to the leaders of the church (Philippians 1:1, 1 Timothy 3), and since there is no other place where their ministry is described, it seems very possible that their origin should be traced to the Seven"[398] here in Acts 6.

Though the question of whether the seven men appointed to serve tables in Acts 6 constitutes the origin of the office of deacons, Saucy presents six convincing arguments that this is the case. First, while these men are not specifically called "deacons," a form of the word is used twice in the passage to describe their work (verse 1, "ministration;" verse 2, "serve"). In addition, the prominent position given by Luke to this incident suggests that he is drawing attention to the creation of a new office. Third, tradition beginning with Irenaeus holds these seven men to be the first deacons. The exacting spiritual qualifications for these seven men also correspond to those listed for the deacon in 1 Timothy 3:8-13. Fifth, if Acts 6 is not the record of the inauguration of deacons, then we have no indication of the start of this new office. Finally, their responsibility of serving tables corresponds to our earliest knowledge of the task of deacons.[399]

Moreover, the expression "serve tables" should not conjure up in the reader's mind thoughts of caterers or table waiters in the restaurant sense. "Tables," τραπηζαι, often denoted "banks," because moneylenders often sat at

---

[398]Kent, 63.

[399]Robert L. Saucy, The Church in God's Program (Chicago: Moody Press, 1972), 154.

tables to conduct their business. The word is so used in Matthew 21:12 and Luke 19:23.[400] In other words, the apostles were not to leave their ministry of the Word to serve as bankers and money-dispensers. This was the job of deacons.

Churches are to have elected officials who are responsible for the church's money. These officials are known as "deacons." Churches are always to have elected officials who are responsible for handling the money given by God's people (2 Corinthians 8:19).

When a Christian gives his money outside of a local church, he is in essence functioning outside of God-ordained authority. God places very serious spiritual qualifications upon the man who handles the offerings of God's people (Acts 6:3). This list of qualifications is exhaustive and demanding (1 Timothy 3:8-13). This is no light matter with God. God wants to make sure that godly men are handling God's money and that this money is distributed properly.

This is a tremendous safeguard to the giving believer. Many things of which a church board is aware, the average Christian misses. There may be many organizations and situations that appear worthy of support but are not. When money is given independent of church authority, God's funds may be misappropriated. To safeguard against this, God has established an ecclesiastical authority within the local church to handle financial matters. The authority is the office of deacon, and the Christian needs to give under that authority. When a believer gives outside of his local church, he is not recognizing God-established authority.

---

[400]Kent, 63.

188

The procedure of missionary giving is through the local church. Church giving protects anonymity, protects continuity, solidifies commitment, and recognizes authority. Where does the giving of the believer belong? It belongs in the local church. This is God's procedure.

The Purpose of Financial Participation

When the Apostle Paul discussed the purpose of missionary giving, he used commercial and financial terms (4:17-18). Paul recalled the generosity of the Philippian church. He had "received" their gift. The papyri gave sufficient evidence that the Greek term απεχω was used as a technical expression for the drawing up of a receipt in business.[401] In other words, Paul was saying, "Here is my receipt."

This thought is further enhanced with the word "abound." This verb translates the Greek term περισσευω, a verb that clearly demonstrates the Philippian gift has more than covered his needs.

He was "full." All his material requirements had been met because of the generosity of the Philippian church. Clearly Paul was grateful. In no way was he guilty of ingratitude or thoughtlessness. After all, if God was pleased with the gift, how could Paul be displeased? The personal satisfaction of the missionary, however, is not the purpose of missionary giving. Paul was very clear that his purpose in writing was not fundraising. He was not seeking a financial gift. "Paul [wanted] it clearly understood that his reason for rejoicing was not because of what he had received materially, but because of the fact that they

---

[401]Martin, 183.

would be rewarded by the God of all grace for their interest in him and attention they had given to him."[402]

Paul disclaimed any covetous seeking of gifts because his concern was for what might have been credited to the Philippian believers' account, not his. The "fruit" on their account refers to accruing interest. The word was frequently used in classical Greek to describe profit from material things, such as flocks, honey, and wool.[403] "What the Philippians gave as their gift was like an investment which would repay rich dividends in the service of the kingdom, as accumulating interest stands to the credit of a depositor."[404] At the Judgment Seat of Christ missionary support will not go unrecognized or unrewarded. The blessing, then, which the Philippian believers gained by giving, was greater than the gift itself. The words of Christ had proven true: "It is more blessed to give than to receive" (Acts 20:35). Missionary giving is a concrete way whereby believers can lay up for themselves treasures in heaven (Matthew 6:19-20).

By giving to missions, the Philippian believers had presented to God a fragrant offering, an offering that was "an odor of a sweet smell" in the nostrils of God (4:18). An understanding of the Greek term οσμη, translated "odor," demands "a knowledge of the ideas of antiquity about

---

[402]Oliver B. Greene, <u>The Epistle of Paul the Apostle to the Philippians</u> (Greenville, SC: The Gospel Hour, 1965), 128.

[403]Mazak, 50.

[404]Martin, 183.

animal and plant physiology."[405] Some in Palestine believed that a withered tree could derive new powers of growth from the scent of waters. Scientific studies do affirm that odors can be "transitional products."[406]

All this provides considerable insight into religious sayings about the "sweet savor" of the gods. Theophanies in religious history often carried the scent of deity. This scent was often "the cause of divine life" or the agent by which divine life was kindled. Even the scent of those who had died was considered to be the force that caused flowers to grow out of their graves.[407]

"The concept of living power given by scents enables" the reader "to understand the Old Testament view that deity inhales the savor of a sacrifice."[408] The savor of sacrifice arouses in deity a favorable disposition toward man (Genesis 8:21). If the sacrifices being offered contained no savor, this was a sign of divine rejection (Leviticus 26:21).[409]

The idea that the scent of sacrifice is pleasing to God is increasingly developed in the New Testament. In the

---

[405]G. Kittel and G. Griedrich, eds., Theological Dictionary of the New Testament, trans. G. W. Bromiley, no. 5 (Grand Rapids: Eerdmans Publishing Company, 1964-68), 493.

[406]Kittel, 493-94.

[407]Kittel, 494.

[408]Kittel, 494.

[409]Kittel, 494.

deepest sense, when Christ offered Himself upon the cross, His self-sacrifice was pleasing to God (Ephesians 5:2).[410] Similarly, the missionary offering of the Philippian church was "an odor of a sweet smell." In other words, just as Christ's atoning sacrifice pleased God, so their financial sacrifice was "well pleasing to God." God found their sacrifice "acceptable" even as He did the sacrifice of His Son.

This is not to say that one can atone for his sins by giving money. There is only one sacrifice that atones for sin, the sacrifice of Christ. The financial sacrifice of the Philippian church, however, was a supreme act of love that pleased the Father, and thus is analogous, though not equivalent, to what Christ did at Calvary. Indeed, one way a believer can prove that he possesses the love of Christ is by giving of himself sacrificially so that others might be saved.

Here, then, is the primary purpose for missionary giving. Missionary giving is a sacrifice that is pleasing to God. "Although financial and transactional terms [were] used of the church's gift, the apostle [also lifted] the minds of his readers above the actual spending and receiving of the gift to the spirit which [had] prompted it and the purpose which it ultimately served."[411] When the believer gives to missions, he does more than promote the cause of Christ and strengthen the hands of God's servants; he engages in an "act of worship in which God takes pleasure."[412] Even the giving of material possessions is "a

---

[410]Kittel, 495.

[411]Martin, 184.

[412]Martin, 184.

spiritual activity."[413] The reward of all service, including stewardship, is "to have pleased" Him.[414]

A Precedent in Financial Participation

The church at Philippi recognized that the entire congregation could not leave Philippi and take their financial gift to the Apostle Paul. An instrument or agent was necessary for this task. The Philippian church chose a man by the name of Epaphroditus to fulfill this need. When Paul received the offering from the church at Philippi, he received it "of Epaphroditus" (4:18). By the Philippian church using an instrument or agent to deliver their money, they set a precedent that later churches have followed. Numerous churches use, and wisely so, a mission board to deliver their offerings to their supported workers. "The Great Commission is far too great a task for any one church without cooperation with other churches of like faith."[415]

For the Sake of Accountability

Epaphroditus delivered the money that the church at Philippi gave to support Paul the missionary. Even today there is nothing wrong with a church giving money to "a middle man" who will deliver the money to the missionary. Churches should be conscious of the fact that missionaries in general are responsible for the raising of all funds relative to their ministries. These funds may be held

---

[413]Mazak, 48.

[414]Martin, 184.

[415]Les Frazier, "Why Choose a Mission Board?" BIMI World, n.d., n.p.

by the treasury department of the mission board from which they can be made available to the missionary. The structure and regulations of the treasury department and field councils control these funds. These regulations avoid unnecessary expenditures and unwise use of funds.[416]

The treasury department of the mission board processes all receipts and donations. Not only does the treasury department receive and process all donations, but it also dispenses the funds according to the direction of the churches and donors. "The main aspect here would be the monthly payment of the missionary's salary and funds for the operation of the work."[417] When one realizes that many missionaries are scattered throughout the world, the complexity of transmitting funds can be well understood.

In addition to financial accountability, mission boards greatly assist in the area of moral accountability. Mission boards provide assurance to local churches that there is oversight, yet not a dictatorial control, over the work being done. Strong missionaries are often independent people who by nature resist accountability. The more powerful a person becomes, the more he may reject the involvement of other people in his life. Even men who start out sincerely seeking to serve God may succumb to the narcotic of power.

Doctrinal accountability is also a provision of the mission board to the local church. History teaches that men

---

[416]Melbourne E. Cuthbert, ed., Managing Missions in the Local Church (Cherry Hill, N.J.: Association of Baptists for World Evangelism, 1987), 157-59.

[417]Cuthbert, 157.

sometimes change their doctrinal positions. When this happens, the men who change their views may not possess enough moral integrity to notify their supporting churches. The field directors of the mission board can be sensitive to this matter and notify the church of a change in a missionary's position. The church can then determine if the change is sufficient enough to warrant the termination of support.

For the Sake of Practicality

Evangelizing the world in light of recent population estimates sometimes "boggles" the mind and frustrates good intentions. What can one local church of any size achieve by carrying on alone? The urgency of reaching the lost world with the sole message of salvation calls for teamwork, cooperation, and proficiency.

"The national and international environment is fraught with political, economic, and cultural upheaval. Missionaries can no longer count on the stability of governments, monetary values, or social orders."[418] Sharing the message of Christ in the context of this hostile atmosphere calls for more than good intentions. Too often local churches and prospective missionaries fail to see the intricacy of the missionary task.

Local churches need assistance in discharging their responsibilities. "Every New Testament church possesses all the self-governing rights and privileges granted by the Lord, but at the same time, one must recognize the physical limitations that restrict any one of them from adequately serving their missionaries and administering the

---

[418]Cuthbert, 43.

work on the field."[419]   It takes the cooperation of local churches to finance and staff God's missionary enterprise. A separate agency devoted to this special ministry can more adequately ascertain the unique needs of each mission field.   Each local church should recognize, commission, and support its own missionaries, but it takes a third party to form the team from different churches.   An approved mission board can and should represent and protect the interests of the churches involved.

Local churches with aggressive missionary programs want to reproduce themselves through the missionaries they send. This objective requires believers committed to the same Biblical distinctives. Without violating the autonomy of the local church, a separate mission agency can make certain that both the missionaries on the team and the work they do accurately comply with the convictions of all who send them.[420]

For the Sake of Identify

A man is judged by the company he keeps. Thus, certain things can be surmised immediately about the missionary candidate by virtue of the board that he selects. The missionary will be seen in a certain light and will be known to have a certain "bent" because he has chosen to affiliate with this particular agency. This judgment, however, is not always negative. By picking the right board, certain things will be affirmed in the life of the missionary.

---

[419]Cuthbert, 44.

[420]Cuthbert, 45.

The Promise Concerning Financial Participation

To the born again believer, there are few verses more precious than Philippians 4:19. The Christian, however, should never divorce this verse from the surrounding context. Obviously, the Christian cannot spend his money frivolously and then claim this truth as his own. There are conditions to be met if one is to rest in the assurance that God will supply all his needs.

"The connection with the preceding verse is given"[421] with the conjunction "but" that begins the verse. The Philippians had apparently helped Paul to their own impoverishment. Paul, however, reassured them that such is not the case. "God will not fail to meet their need as they have not been remiss in meeting his."[422] The faithfulness of God was being stressed in emphatic words. Just as God was able to supply the needs of the missionary through his supporting churches, so God would supply the needs of that supporting church because of their sacrificial participation in world evangelism. "Those who give to missionary outreach will be rewarded."[423]

God's supply is predominantly thought of here in financial terms. The phrase "will supply" translates the Greek term πληρωσει, which is the same term translated "I am full" in verse 18. Moreover, the word "need" in this verse translates the same Greek term that was used of the apostle's "necessity" in verse 16. Clearly, then, Paul was inferring that because they had met their financial

---

[421]Martin, 184.

[422]Martin, 184.

[423]Martin, 48.

obligation to him, God would be careful to see that their financial obligations were met.

It would be wrong, however, "to exclude the thought of the provision of God for their spiritual needs"[424] as well. This is made clear by the apostle's choice of words, namely, that God would supply "all their need." Whatever their deficiency might have been, financial or spiritual, God would supply the remedy.

Perhaps the words "my God" imply that the Apostle Paul had proven this principle to be true in his personal history. "He did not hesitate to make it clear that to him, God was a personal friend."[425] Evidently Paul had proven God to be valid on more than one occasion. Paul was confident that God would not disappoint the Philippian believers in the full supply of their needs, whatever they might have been.

The source and extent of this divine supply are given with the profound words "according to his riches in glory by Christ Jesus" (4:19). Paul's choice of prepositions here clearly reveals that the "rewarding will not be merely from His wealth, but also in a manner that befits His wealth — on a scale worthy of His wealth."[426] "Oh the depth of riches both of the wisdom and knowledge of God! (Romans 11:33).

These riches are glorious indeed. The exact force of the phrase "in glory" (4:19) has been variously

---

[424]Martin, 185.

[425]Greene, 130.

[426]Martin, 185.

understood. Some have seen the phrase in an adverbial sense. God will supply one's needs in a glorious manner. Others have understood the phrase as a reference to the glory reserved for believers in heaven, that is, in the glory. Perhaps the best interpretation, however, sees the phrase as modifying the word "riches." This understanding accords well with Old Testament usage where the words "riches" and "glory" are used synonymously (Genesis 31:1, Isaiah 10:3). These are glorious riches.[427]

Thus the one who gives to missions receives glorious riches "by Christ Jesus" (4:19). "We know that every good and perfect gift comes from God. Our temporal needs are met through the riches of Christ Jesus."[428] All that the Christian has and enjoys is because of Christ. "In him, God's full wealth of revelation and redemption is contained, so that we are rich in him."[429] Because a Christian is in union with Christ, he is linked to the source and supply of all true wealth. This wealth of Christ is promised to the one who sacrificially gives to missions.

The Privilege of Financial Participation

As Paul concluded his missionary letter by thanking the Philippian believers for their financial participation in his gospel ministry, he burst into a doxology of praise to God (4:20). Praise was rendered to the Father for His goodness and grace, Paul's way of thanking God for the response of the Philippian believers who met his need and participated with him in the work of missions. The

---

[427]Martin, 185.

[428]Greene, 130.

[429]Martin, 185.

"Amen" that concludes the verse is derived from a Hebrew verb that means "to be firm." This word "underlies the truth of the doxology, as the writer and reader associate themselves with the confession and own it as valid and true for themselves."[430] It is a privilege to be involved in the missionary enterprise physically and financially, and Paul praised the Lord for this privilege.

Without the sharing of the Gospel message, there would be no such thing as authentic Christian fellowship. It is the work of missions that crease saints and Christian brothers (4:21). Frequently throughout the Philippian correspondence Paul was careful "to include the whole Christian community at Philippi within the scope of his pastoral care,"[431] and the close of the letter is no exception. As Paul thought about the saints, he was reminded of those who were with him, especially those "that [were] of Caesar's household" (4:22). The occasion of mentioning them "may conceivably have been the link of special interest between the Christian members of the imperial staff in government service at the place of Paul's imprisonment and the Christian citizens of Philippi which was a Roman colony."[432] Indeed, there is a bond between those who are in the body of Christ wherever they may be found, and it is the privilege of missionary work to add members to the brotherhood. This is all made possible by the "grace of our Lord Jesus Christ" (4:23). This is Paul's prayer for those who are at Philippi.

---

[430]Martin, 186.

[431]Martin, 186.

[432]Martin, 186.

A Summary Application for the Local Church

"Eight out of every ten dollars held by Christians in the world are in the hands of Americans."[433] God has blessed Americans for the purpose of world evangelism (Psalm 67:1-2). It is imperative, therefore, that American believers increase their vision to include the world.

Financial participation in missions is a wonderful privilege. Unfortunately, American Christians still speak of "taking" an offering and "paying" tithes. Such terminology betrays a miserly heart and resentment toward giving. When God speaks of giving, He uses terms that speak of "securing a sound investment"[434] rather than paying a bill.[435]

The local church that gives to missions in the fashion outlined in Philippians 4 will be rewarded tremendously. Those who concretely take this chapter's contents at face value will experience the providential blessing of God. May every Christian who has read these pages be encouraged to give "over and above the tithe with faith in the promises of God to multiply the gift so as to supply the need of the giver so he in turn may give even more."[436]

---

[433]Neal Pirolo, <u>Serving as Senders</u> (San Diego: Emmaus Road, International, 1991), 76.

[434]Pirolo, 78.

[435]For example, Malachi 3:10 and Matthew 6:20.

[436]W. Eugene Gurganus, <u>Investing for Eternity</u> (Cherry Hill, NJ: Association of Baptists for World Evangelism, n.d.), 32.

Appendix A
What Did the Executives Say?

This book has proposed an instrument whereby local churches can evaluate missionaries that they are considering for financial support. The instrument, because it was based on the book of Philippians, was intended to do more than just evaluate the missionary's philosophy of ministry. The instrument was designed to reveal more about the missionary himself. The premise ran throughout the book that many problems exist on the mission field, not because of deficient philosophies and ministry practices, but because of deficient character in missionaries. Various chapters within the book dealt with personal issues gleaned from the book of Philippians.

A Summary of the Instrument

Chapter two dealt with interpersonal relationships. The premise in this chapter is that interpersonal conflict causes many missionaries to leave the field earlier than planned. It is therefore necessary for the missionary to have solid relationships. His primary relationship is to Jesus Christ, but good relationships must also exist between the missionary and his fellow workers. In addition, the missionary must seek solid relationships with the nationals he is seeking to reach and with the churches who are supporting his missionary endeavors.

Chapter three concentrated on surrender and commitment. Often the missionary who struggles with interpersonal relationships drops out of missionary service prematurely. Exegesis reveals that in order to maintain a strong commitment level to missions, the missionary must develop an appreciative love for the people he has been called to reach. It was discovered that this appreciative love is often maintained through an aggressive prayer life for one's target audience. In addition, the missionary must recognize that God allows certain things to happen in the lives of His servants so that He may perfect the good work that He has begun in them. In short, the ability to think of others rather than one's self often governs one's commitment to missions.

Chapter four focused on the prayer life of the missionary. It is imperative for missionaries to maintain a personal devotional life. This necessitates praying with proper motives, for pure prayer has a way of binding hearts together. The instrument asserts that missionaries will have a clearer understanding of each other if they have a greater spiritual vision of God. God's resources that enable the missionary to do his work are released through prayer. Indeed, no stage of the missionary's work is victorious without prayer.

Chapter five focused attention to the contentment level of missionaries. Here it was argued that the economic gap that exists between missionaries and nationals makes friendship virtually impossible. Evangelistic efforts are enhanced when the Gospel is placed over personal comfort. In short, missionary life is a life of suffering and denial; the missionary's personal desires must be subordinated to his ministerial responsibilities.

Chapter six stressed the importance of the missionary's pulpit ministry. The instrument stressed that the work of missions is tied to effective preaching. The missionary should seek through his pulpit ministry to stress harmonious church relationships against worldly pagan influences. He should also use his pulpit to encourage church members to exercise humility when confronted with others in the church who have divergent personal ideas. Here it was also stressed that the missionary should use the example of Jesus to illustrate his sermons. In addition, missionary preachers should seek to apply Biblical truth to their audiences.

Chapter seven dealt with the missionary's planning for the future. To be a successful missionary, one must have a vision for the future, and this necessitates the establishment of goals. Missionaries who succeed are those who are characterized by sane, rational decisions, which require proper planning. Proper planning always seeks to use people. When proper planning is not done, the missionary becomes weary and troubled. Missionaries must prioritize their schedules and function according to these priorities. It must be recognized, however, that missionaries sometimes have to alter their plans so that God's plan can be accomplished.

Chapter eight concentrated on the educational background of the missionary. Proper missionary preparation relieves some of the stress of arriving on the field. Though this education may improve the missionary's learning ability, the primary purpose is to deepen his spiritual life. In addition, secular education, while having some detrimental factors, could be pertinent to missionary work. It was also discovered that nontraditional education has much to commend it, but this must be done in addition to, never in lieu of, "old-fashioned book learning." If the missionary is not careful, however, his advanced degrees can cause him to be useless on the mission field because education can lead to reliance upon professional qualifications rather than on the Spirit of God.

Chapter nine discusses the missionary's philosophy of separation. This separation must always be practiced in love. Separation itself can never be repudiated as a strategy because Scripture commands it. The missionary can be motivated to separation by remembering that this world is not his final place of residence.

Chapter ten deals with the local church's financial participation in worthy missionaries. If finances were not required, many of God's people would miss their opportunity to invest in world evangelism. Such investment begins with love, joy, and peace in the Christian's heart. When Christians give to missions, more churches are planted, and the Word of God is advanced. This mission giving should be done through the auspices of a local, New Testament church. These local churches, however, should use mission boards for the sake of accountability, practicality, and identity. Christians should give to missions because such sacrifices please God. The Lord will meet the needs of those who sacrificially give to missions. Christians should view missionary giving as a privilege.

The Method of the Evaluation

The prongs of the instrument were placed into the form of forty-eight summary statements that were sent along with a cover letter to various mission executives. Three representatives each were chosen from the Association of Baptists for World Evangelism, Baptist International Missions, Inc., Baptist Mid-Missions, and Baptist World Mission. With each board, the president and/or general director was chosen because of his extensive understanding of Baptist missionary work. In addition, one expert from each board in the field of education was chosen, as well as one expert in the area of missionary relations.

Each mission executive was asked to evaluate the forty-eight statements individually by checking the squares that best expressed his sentiment. The boxes were marked "strongly agree," "agree," "do not know," "disagree," and "strongly disagree." "These five positions were given simple weights of 5, 4, 3, 2, and 1 for scoring purposes."[437] Having scored each item from 5 to 1, the item scores were added to produce a total score. Statements for which there was no response were not tabulated in the results.

Of the 564 statements for which there was a response, there was a cumulative point total of 2,414. This produced an average of 4.28 per answer indicating that the experts agreed with the instrument overall.[438] This agreement with the instrument overall, however, does not indicate how the experts felt about the various individual prongs of the instrument.

An Analysis of the Data

To better understand the sentiment of the evaluators, it is necessary to evaluate the data prong by prong. This requires analyzing the data according to the various chapter divisions of the book, starting with the underlying

---

[437]A. N. Oppenheim, Questionnaire Design and Attitude Measurement (London: Heinemann Educational Books, 1966), 133.

[438]For exact point totals per respondent, see Appendix B.

premise of the research question and working through the various subsidiary questions.

Underlying Premise

The underlying premise throughout the dissertation is that numerous problems exist on the mission field, not because of deficient philosophies and ministry practices, but because of deficient character in missionaries. Five of the twelve missionary executives surveyed disagreed with this premise, while four agreed and two strongly agreed. One did not answer the question because he felt that "both were true." Another respondent who disagreed felt similarly stating, "They all cause problems." One of the respondents who disagreed felt that the premise was "over simplified." Another disagreeing respondent added that "character problems do exist," but he "would not qualify them as numerous." There seemed to be some divergence among the executives as to the validity of the premise, leading to an average score of 3.27. This divergence reveals that there is some disagreement among Baptist missionary executives as to the premise of this book. Hopefully this work will make a significant contribution to this ongoing debate.

Interpersonal Relationships

Chapter two deals with interpersonal relationships, and the underlying premise of this chapter is that interpersonal conflict causes many missionaries to leave the field earlier than planned. Eight of the twelve executives agreed with this premise, and two strongly agreed. One of the respondents who agreed stated, "Problems are not necessarily caused by deficient character. Sometimes they are caused by two individuals with strong character, but with different viewpoints" like "Paul and Barnabas." Another who agreed with the premise felt that it would be better to say that some, rather than many missionaries, leave the field prematurely because of interpersonal conflict. There were only two men who disagreed with the premise. The average score for this tenet was 3.83.

It is argued in chapter two that the strongest credential any missionary can carry to the field is an intimacy with Jesus Christ. Eleven of the twelve executives strongly agreed with this, while one only agreed because he felt that the assertion does not "exclude Biblical obedience." The average score for this statement was 4.92.

Chapter two also emphasizes unity among missionary workers and the fact that this unity could not be stressed too strongly. Eight of the executives surveyed strongly agreed with this assertion and three more agreed. One did not answer the question because he felt there should have been some explanations as to whether the missionary workers under discussion were with "the same board" or "similar boards." He asked whether missionaries were expected to bridge "theological and philosophical differences" merely for the sake of unity. The average score for this statement was 4.73.

When it comes to interpersonal relationships with the lost, chapter two argues that the missionary must develop meaningful relationships with local people from the very first day on the field. There was not much disagreement among the executives on this assumption. Nine of the twelve strongly agreed with the proposal, while the remaining three agreed. This produced a high score of 4.75.

The remaining interpersonal issue pertained to missionaries and their supporting churches. This chapter asserts that missionaries must sense a certain amount of accountability to those from whom they receive support. Once again there was not much disagreement among the executives. Eleven of the twelve executives strongly agreed and one agreed. An extremely high score of 4.92 was registered.

Surrender and Commitment

Chapter three discusses surrender and commitment. The underlying premise throughout this chapter was that the missionaries who cause the greatest problems are often those who will eventually drop out of missionary service. Eight of the mission executives surveyed agreed with this premise and one strongly agreed. Two did not know, and one disagreed. The one who disagreed stated, "Some independent personalities have great longevity" and thus the premise is "not necessarily" true. One of the agreeing executives concurred stating, "At times persistent problem-makers spend their entire career on the mission field." One executive added perspective with his comment that it is "unresolved problems" that cause missionaries to leave the field. Another executive added, "Sometimes this is due to personality problems, lack of preparation, and immaturity." He stated, "We have seen some who were never called of God to serve overseas destroy themselves, their families, colleagues and nationals on the field." The average response to this statement was 3.75.

To remain committed to the task of world evangelism, chapter three argues that the missionary must develop a strong appreciative love for the people he has been called to reach. There was not much disagreement here. Ten of the twelve missionary executives strongly agreed and two agreed producing an average score of 4.83.

209

Chapter three also argues that the missionary quickly finds his heart departing from the people for whom he has failed to pray. Six of the executives agreed with this, and the remaining six strongly agreed. One of the agreeing respondents, however, stated, "It is possible that a missionary could love his people and not pray sufficiently for them." The average score for this prong of the instrument was 4.50.

Another important ingredient in the commitment level of the missionary is a recognition of the sovereignty of God. The missionary must recognize that God is a sovereign God who allows certain things to happen in the lives of His servants so that He may perfect the good work He began in them. Nine of the respondents strongly agreed, while three agreed. Once again a high average score was registered, in this case 4.75.

The final assertion in the area of surrender and commitment was that these areas are governed by one's ability to think of others rather than himself. Six agreed with the assertion, and the remaining six strongly agreed. This produced an average score of 4.50.

Prayer Life

The prayer life of the missionary was the concentration of chapter four. Here it was stressed that it is imperative for missionaries to maintain a personal devotional life. All twelve respondents strongly agreed with this assertion, giving this prong of the instrument the highest rating possible, a 5.00.

Chapter four was quick to add, however, that the missionary will experience spiritual poverty and powerlessness in prayer if he prays with the wrong motives. Five of the executives surveyed agreed with this assertion, while the remaining seven strongly agreed. Thus, another high average score was given, in this instance 4.58. As one respondent put it, "This tenet is not only true of missionaries; it is true of everyone."

One of the reasons that pure prayer is imperative is that it binds hearts together. Once again there was not much disagreement among the respondents. Seven executives strongly agreed with this assertion, and five agreed. Once again the average score was 4.58.

Chapter four went on to stress that missionaries will have a clearer understanding of each other if they have a greater spiritual vision of God. The average score here dropped slightly. Seven executives agreed, while only five strongly agreed. The score was 4.42.

Another reason for prayer is effective ministry. God's resources that enable the missionary to do God's work are released through prayer. Seven executives strongly agreed with this proposition, while five agreed. One of the respondents who agreed added the qualifying word "sometimes." The average score rose to 4.58.

The chapter on prayer was summarized by stating that no stage of the missionary's work is victorious without prayer. While most of the executives responded favorably to this assertion, there were a few dissenting voices. Nine strongly agreed, one agreed, one did not know, and one disagreed. The average score was 4.50. The respondent who stated that he did not know replied, "Some successful missionaries have proven to be less than spiritual." The disagreeing executive had a similar thought. "There are certain stages of a missionary's work that could be successful without prayer." Building and language study were listed as examples. The mission executive stated that he "would agree that greater success could be achieved through prayer, but some success can be gained without it. Judas Iscariot was certainly a successful disciple, yet lost."

Contentment

The assumption of chapter five is that missionaries ought to be content with less income. It was here that the missionary executives took the greatest exception to the instrument. A premise ran throughout this chapter that the economic gap that exists between missionaries and nationals makes friendship virtually impossible. One respondent did not know, while seven disagreed and four strongly disagreed. The average score was very low here, registering only a 1.75. Two executives felt that the word "sometimes" should be added, but others were more critical. One stated, "This is a view widely-held, but not grounded in fact." Another stated that this assumption "is not taught in Philippians as I read it, and I have found that national believers in third-world countries accept and even expect their missionaries to live in houses with water and electricity, even if they themselves are living in huts because they know the missionaries will be stronger for the work and stay longer that way than if they lowered their standard of living to abject poverty levels." He went on to say, "The nationals know when something is done for effect and when it is done out of necessity, and missionaries who lowered their standard of living for effect would lose respect among nationals."

Ironically, however, these same executives responded favorably to the statement that that the ability to place the Gospel over personal comfort provides a great enhancement to evangelistic efforts. Eight respondents said that they agreed with this, and four strongly agreed, producing an average score of 4.33.

When asked if missionary life was one of suffering and denial, the executives gave a wide spectrum of answers. The average score was 2.67, but there was no consensus as to the validity of this proposition. Four agreed, two did not know, four disagreed, and two strongly disagreed. One of the agreeing executives felt that the word "sometimes" would be a necessary qualifier. A disagreeing respondent expressed a similar thought when he wrote, "Missionaries must be prepared to suffer, but not all do suffer." Another stated, "Having served ten years as a missionary in Peru, I did not see my life as one of suffering and denial. I believe that when one has surrendered his life and will to God, He gives that missionary the desires he should have and so there is no denial. It is a privilege to serve God, not a hardship." This thought may have prompted at least one executive to answer that he did not know. His response stated, "This needs much clarification. In light of Philippians 1:27ff, yes."

When asked if the missionary's personal desires should be subordinated to his personal responsibilities, once again there was divergence of opinion. Seven agreed with this statement, and one strongly agreed. Two, however, disagreed, and one did not know. This produced an average score of 3.64. The executive who strongly agreed said that the statement was true in the sense that all Christians must die to self. An executive who disagreed said that this subordination must take place only if personal desires and ministerial responsibilities were in conflict. One executive chose not to respond, and he did so because he felt the phrase "personal desires" was too ambiguous. He stated, "If you are referring to things such as personal conflicts, hobbies, etc. I would agree. On the other, hand if

his desires are to be with family, [or for] personal enrich-
ment, etc. I would disagree."

Pulpit Ministry

The sixth chapter of the book deals with pulpit ministry. The premise ran throughout this chapter that the work
of missions is tied to effective preaching. Once again
there was much divergence. Two executives strongly
agreed, though one of them did question what was meant
by the word "effective." Five respondents agreed, but one
qualified his response with the word "sometimes" and
added that he knows of "great missionaries who can't
preach." Another agreeing respondent added that this is
true, but other ministries must supplement preaching. He
stated insightfully, "First you must have an audience."
Five respondents, however, disagreed with the premise.
One disagreeing respondent stated, "Some very poor
preachers have made great missionaries. It's effective
communication that's needed." The score for this premise
was 3.33.

The chapter on pulpit ministry went on to discuss the
content of the missionary's sermons. It was argued that
missionaries should stress the importance of harmonious
church relationships against worldly pagan influences.
The score here was high. Eight of the respondents agreed,
and three strongly agreed. One, however, answered that
he did not know because the question was "unclear." The
average score was 4.17.

Chapter six also argued that a missionary's sermon
content should stress the importance of Christians exercising humility when confronted with others in the church
who have divergent personal ideas. Once again there was
a general consensus. Eight responded that they agreed,

who strongly agreed added that this tenet was "very Biblical." One executive, however, disagreed with the statement. The average score was 4.08.

In order to be effective, preaching must use illustrations. Exegesis in Philippians revealed that Paul chose to use the illustration of Jesus Christ. It was argued that Christ is the most powerful illustration a preacher can use. There was a slight disagreement among the respondents. Seven strongly agreed with this hypothesis, and three agreed. One, however, stated that he did not know, while another said that he disagreed. The average score was 4.33.

The final prong in the chapter on pulpit ministry dealt with the necessity of application. Missionary preachers should always seek to apply Biblical truth in their sermons. This belief elicited overwhelming agreement. It received a high mark of 4.75, with nine strongly agreeing and three agreeing.

Vision for the Future

A vision for the future was the focus of chapter seven, and the underlying thought was that in order for missionaries to be successful, they must have a vision for the future, which necessitates the establishment of goals. There was much consensus on this point. Five executives responded that they strongly agreed, and the remaining seven agreed. This produced a high score of 4.42.

It was similarly argued that the missionaries who succeed are characterized by sane, rational decisions, which necessitate proper planning. Again, the consensus was strong. Nine agreed with the premise, and three strongly agreed. This produced a score of 4.25. One executive, however, insightfully added, "Believe it or not, some of the most successful missionaries are not great organizers or planners, but are more spontaneous in their style of ministry."

The chapter on planning went on to emphasize that proper planning always seeks to use people. Four of the executives strongly agreed with this proposition, though one did question the use of the word "utilize." Another seven agreed, but one disagreed. The average score was 4.17.

The book presents the idea that all too often missionaries become troubled and weary because they have not prioritized their schedules and functioned according to these priorities. The average score here was 4.25. Six agreed, and five strongly agreed, with one even throwing in a qualifying "Amen!" One executive, however, chose to disagree stating that the missionary "is just as likely to be frustrated over a plan that proved impossible to follow."

His dissent expresses the sentiment of the final prong in the chapter on planning. Missionaries need to recognize when it is necessary to alter their plans in order that the plan of God might be done. Most executive recognized that there was a need to bow to the sovereignty of God in the area of planning. Two agreed with proposal, and an overwhelming ten strongly agreed with one even offering Proverbs 16:9 as a proof text. The average score here was 4.83.

Educational Background

Chapter eight discussed education as it relates to the missionary. The researcher believes that proper missionary preparation relieves some of the stress of arriving on the field. The executives who were surveyed tended to agree with this assumption. Seven of the twelve strongly agreed, with the remaining five agreeing. The average score was 4.58.

There was some divergence, however, as to the express purpose of this education. Three strongly agreed with the premise that although education should improve the missionary's learning ability, the primary purpose is to deepen his spiritual walk. Another six agreed with this proposition. Three, however, chose to disagree. One of the disagreeing executives stated, "Education has to do with imparting knowledge and that may or may not deepen the spiritual life." Another dissenter said, "Spirituality is more important than education, but the purpose of education is education. Christian education also emphasizes Christian values and personal spirituality." The average score for this question was 3.75.

Most of the executives surveyed, however, did feel that secular education, though having detrimental factors, could be pertinent to missionary life. The average score here was 4.27. Eight agreed with this suggestion, and another strongly agreed. One, however, chose not to answer the question, stating that this was true only if one were talking about mechanics rather than mentality.

When asked if advanced degrees can cause the careless missionary to be useless on the field, there was a wide divergence of opinion among the executives. One strongly agreed stating that this "can happen anywhere." Another five agreed with this thought. Four, however, chose to disagree with it. One of the disagreeing executives stated that "this is not a documentable cause to effect." Another disagreeing respondent added, "It is the problem of carelessness, not the degrees." One executive chose to strongly disagree with the proposition, while two others chose not to answer. One who chose not to answer stated that this was possible, but the "issue would be character and common sense, not degrees of education." The remaining executive who chose not to answer stated that "each case is different." The average score here was 3.20.

Philosophy of Separation

Chapter nine discusses the issue of separation. The premise is that when the missionary practices separation, it complements his evangelism. Five of the executives surveyed strongly agreed with this premise, while another six agreed. One of the agreeing respondents added the word "Biblical" to separation stating, "Sometimes Biblical separation is confused with personal and cultural preferences." The average score for the premise was 4.45. One respondent chose not to answer any questions on the issue of separation because he was "uncertain" as to what was meant by the term.

An overwhelming ten respondents strongly agreed with the idea that love is an important and necessary prerequisite to separation. The remaining respondent who answered agreed. This produced a very high average score of 4.91.

Similarly, most of executives concurred with the fact that separation cannot be repudiated as a strategy because Scripture commands it. Seven of the respondents strongly agreed with this assessment, while another four agreed. The average score was 4.64.

Finally, the missionary executives were asked to evaluate the hypothesis that a missionary is motivated to separation when he remembers that this world is not his final place of residence. Five of the respondents agreed with this, while another five strongly agreed. One of the executives who strongly agreed, however, stated that the statement was "true," but that this is "not the only or even primary motivation." Another respondent disagreed with the statement because he believes that "God's holiness is the motivation." The average score for this proposition was 4.27.

Financial Participation

The last chapter of the instrument deals with the church's financial participation in worthy missionary candidates. Here the premise states that if finances were not required, many of God's people would miss their opportunity to invest in world evangelism. Five executives agreed with this premise, while another four strongly agreed. Two responded that they did not know, while a remaining respondent refused to answer stating that this was "true from a practical standpoint, but not necessarily so." The average score of the premise was 4.18.

The chapter on financial participation also argues that Christians give more to missions when love, joy, and peace characterize their hearts. The executives tended to concur. Six of the respondents strongly agreed, while the remaining six agreed. The average score for this proposal was 4.50.

The chapter also argues that when Christians give to missions, more churches are planted and the Word of God is increased. There was a somewhat divergent opinion among the executives as to the validity of this statement. Four strongly agreed, and six agreed. One of the agreeing respondents stated, however, that this "depends on how funds are used. Orphanages are expensive too." Another respondent agreed stating that the proposition was true "if the dollars are spent properly." This stipulation caused him to answer that he did not know. A final respondent disagreed with the statement altogether stating that it is true "only if the gifts are stewarded with that end in view." The average score for this statement was 4.08.

Chapter ten also argues that missions giving should be done through the auspices of a local, New Testament church. Surprisingly, nine of these men who affiliated with para-church organizations strongly agreed, while the remaining three agreed. One of those who agreed felt that giving should be done primarily through a church, though not exclusively. The average score was 4.75.

The same average score was registered for the use of mission boards. When asked if churches increase accountability, practicality, and identity by using mission boards, the executives obviously concurred. Nine strongly agreed, and the remaining three agreed. It stands to reason that those affiliated with mission boards would be so inclined.

Chapter ten also argues that Christians should give to missions primarily because such sacrifices please God. Five strongly agreed with this statement, and another six agreed. One of those who agreed questioned the use of the word "primarily." Another respondent chose not to answer the question at all because he felt missionary giving was primarily an act of obedience. The average score for this tenet was 4.45.

God will meet the needs of those who sacrificially give to missions. This was another assertion of the chapter on financial participation, and most of the executives supported this finding. The average score was 4.42. Seven strongly agreed, and four more agreed. One, however, chose to disagree stating that "there is nothing magical about missions giving. God loves His children regardless of their giving practices."

The final prong of the instrument states that Christians should view missionary giving as a privilege. The instrument ended on a high note with ten of the twelve respondents strongly agreeing, while the remaining two agreed. The average score was 4.83.

The Conclusion of the Dissertation

With a few minor exceptions, the researcher was pleased with the responses that he received from the mission executives. All were punctual and helpful with their responses. Many were encouraging and supportive. The researcher's only regret can be summarized in the statement of one executive who said, "It would have been useful to discuss some of the answers given with you personally. Past experience and opinions are probably mixed in some of the answers given."

Even those who were critical of the instrument at points forced the researcher to go back and re-evaluate the findings. For example, one executive wrote, "Commonly held false notions should not be made to appear to flow from the text of Philippians." Indeed, the executive is right. In his case he took tremendous exception to the premise that the economic gap that exists between missionaries and nationals makes friendship virtually impossible. He was not alone. Most executives took exception to this prong of the instrument, and this caused the researcher to do much soul searching. Ironically, however, one executive who strongly disagreed with the tenet of the instrument recommended a book that argued the other way. Indeed, this recommended book was the one that convinced this author that economic divergence is a problem on the mission field.

One stated that "the wording of most of these assertions would change if the author could speak from actual missionary experience. Hypotheses prevail here." Indeed, the author does have much to learn about actual missionary experience, but this should not call into question his love for missions and missionaries.

As stated in the introduction, there was a three-fold purpose for this book. It was designed to be a missiological commentary on the book of Philippians. It was designed to be an evaluative tool for missionaries going to the field, and it was designed to be a helpful aid in assisting local churches in their evaluation of missionary candidates. To the degree that this book positively helps in these areas, it is successful.

May the reader and the author be strengthened in those areas where unanimity exists and constructively debate where there are areas of robust disagreement. May the goal of each be the glorification of Christ and the advancement of His church. To God be the glory.

Appendix B
Table of Mission Executive Responses

Name of Executive	Name of Board[439]	Total Score	Number of Questions Answered	Average Per Question
Gary Anderson	BMM	186	48	3.88
Brian Burkholder	BIMI	187	43	4.35
David Cummins	BWM	188	45	4.18
Jesse Eaton	ABWE	200	48	4.58
Leslie Frazier	BIMI	220	48	4.58
Steve Fulks	BMM	198	48	4.13
Paul Holritz	ABWE	222	48	4.63
Wendell Kempton	ABWE	189	48	3.94
Fred Moritz	BWM	217	48	4.52
Don Sisk	BIMI	198	48	4.13
William Smallman	BMM	216	48	4.50
Dennis Walton	BWM	193	44	4.39
Totals		2,414	564	4.28

[439]ABWE=Association of Baptist for World Evangelism; BIMI=Baptist International Missions, Inc.; BMM=Baptist Mid-Missions; BWM=Baptist World Mission.

Bibliography

Allen, Roland, <u>Missionary Methods: Paul's or Ours?</u>.
Grand Rapids: Eerdmans Publishing Company, 1962.

The Bible. Authorized King James Version.

Bonk, Jonathan J. <u>Missions and Money</u>. Maryknoll, NY:
Orbis Books, 1991.

Broadus, John A. <u>On the Preparation and Delivery of
Sermons</u>. San Francisco: Harper Collins, 1979.

Campbell, Robert J. "The Program for Pre-Field
Orientation for Appointees of Greater Europe
Mission." D.Min. diss., Trinity Evangelical Divinity
School, 1987.

Cannon, Joseph L. <u>For Missionaries Only</u>. Grand Rapids:
Baker Book House, 1969.

Collins, Marjorie. <u>Manual for Today's Missionaries</u>.
Pasadena, CA: William Carey Library, 1972.

Cuthbert, Melbourne, ed. <u>Managing Missions in the Local
Church</u>. Cherry Hill, NJ: Association of Baptists for
World Evangelism, 1987.

Devries, Hendrik. "A Missionary's Economic Decision-
Making in the Context of Disparity." Th.M. diss.,
Calvin Theological Seminary, 1989.

Dowdy, J. Paul. "The Problem of Missionary Volunteer
Drop-Outs." <u>Grace Journal</u> 7 (1966): 22-25.

Engel, James F., and Wilbert Norton. What's Gone
 Wrong with the Harvest? Grand Rapids: Zondervan
 Publishing House, 1975.

Francis, T. Dayanandan. "Gospel and Communications."
 Arasaradi Journal of Theological Reflection 5, no. 1
 (1992): 133-34.

Frazier, Les. "Why Choose a Mission Board?" BIMI
 World, n.d.: n.p.

Gilliland, Dean S. Pauline Theology and Mission Practice.
 Grand Rapids: Baker Book House, 1983.

Golz, Lud. "If Paul Got Organized to Reach His
 Objectives, So Can You." Evangelical Missions
 Quarterly 27, no. 3 (1991): 268-72.

Greene, Oliver B. The Epistle of Paul the Apostle to the
 Philippians. Greenville, SC: The Gospel Hour, 1965.

Gurganus, W. Eugene. Investing for Eternity. Cherry
 Hill, NJ: Association of Baptists for World
 Evangelism, n.d.

Guyon, Madame. Experiencing God through Prayer.
 Springdale, PA: Whitaker House, 1984.

Hale, Thomas. On Being a Missionary: Pasadena, CA:
 William Carey Library, 1995.

Hiebert, D. Edmond. An Introduction to the Pauline
 Epistles. Chicago: Moody Press, 1954.

Hiebert, Paul. Anthropological Insights for Missionaries.
 Grand Rapids: Baker Book House, 1987.

Iwasko, Ronald. "A Personnel Director Speaks to Professors of Mission." Paper presented at the Evangelical Theological Society, 42nd National Conference, New Orleans, LA, 15-17 November 1990.

Jackson, Foakes, and Kirsoppp Lake. <u>The Acts of the Apostles</u>. Part 1 of <u>The Beginnings of Christianity</u>. 5 vols. London: Macmillan and Company, 1920.

Kaiser, Walter C., and Moises Silva. <u>An Introduction to Biblical Hermeneutics</u>. Grand Rapids: Zondervan Publishing House, 1994.

Kane, Herbert J. <u>The Making of a Missionary</u>. Grand Rapids: Baker Book House, 1975.

Kent, Homer A. <u>Jerusalem to Rome</u>. Grand Rapids: Baker Book House, 1972.

King, Guy H. <u>New Order</u>. Fort Washington, PA: Christian Literature Crusade, 1943.

Kittel, G. and G. Friedrich, eds. <u>Theological Dictionary of the New Testament</u>. Trans. G. W. Bromiley, no. 5. Grand Rapids: Eerdmans Publishing Company, 1980.

Lee, David T.W. "A Missionary Training Program for University Students in South Korea." D.Miss. diss., Trinity Evangelical Divinity School, 1983.

Lim, Kyung Taeg. "A Comparative Analysis of Programming and Budgeting for Mission Fund Development in Local Churches of Kwangju, Kyunggi Province, Korea." D.Miss., diss., Western Seminary, 1999.

Lingenfelter, Sherwood. Agents of Transformation. Grand Rapids: Baker Book House, 1996.

Lockyer, Herbert. All the Men of the Bible. Grand Rapids: Zondervan Publishing House, 1958.

Lunde, Joel S. "Curriculum Proposals in Mission for the Lutheran Brethren Seminary." D.Miss. diss., Trinity Evangelical Divinity School, 1985.

Lush, Ron. "Committed to Serve, Prepared to Lead: A Leadership Development Curriculum for International and Cross-Cultural Christian Ministry Leadership." D.Miss. diss., Trinity Evangelical Divinity School, 1985.

MacArthur, John, Jr. Charismatic Chaos. Grand Rapids: Zondervan Publishing House, 1992.

---. Romans 1-8. Chicago: Moody Press, 1991.

---. Romans 9-16. Chicago: Moody Press, 1994.

Marshall, I. Howard. The Acts of the Apostles. Grand Rapids: Eerdmans Publishing Company, 1980.

Martin, Ralph P. The Epistle of Paul to the Philippians. Grand Rapids: Eerdmans Publishing Company, 1987.

Mazak, Gregory J. "The Peace of the Christian Life." Biblical Viewpoint 26, no. 1 (1992), 41-51.

McCutcheon, Nancy S. "The Importance of Spiritual, Psychological, Academic, and Skills Preparation for Missionary Candidates." M.A. diss., Columbia Biblical Seminary, 1993.

McLachlan, Douglas R. Reclaiming Authentic Fundamentalism. Independence, MO: American Association of Christian Schools, 1993.

Moritz, Fred. Be Ye Holy. Greenville, SC: Bob Jones University Press, 1994.

Murray, Andrew. With Christ in the School of Prayer. Grand Rapids: Zondervan Publishing House, 1983.

Neil, William. Acts. Grand Rapids: Eerdmans Publishing Company, 1973.

O'Brien, Peter T. "The Fellowship Theme in Philippians." Reformed Theological Review 37, no. 1 (1978): 9-18.

O'Donnell, Kelly S., and Michele Lewis O'Donnell, eds. Helping Missionaries Grow. Pasadena, CA: William Carey Library, 1988.

Oppenheim, A. N. Questionnaire Design and Attitude Measurement. London: Heinemann Books, 1966.

Packer, J. I. Knowing God. Downers Grove, IL: InterVarsity Press, 1973.

Pache, Rene'. The Inspiration and Authority of Scripture. Trans. Helen I. Needham. Salem, WI: Sheffield Publishing Company, 1992.

Palmer, Donald C. "Development of a Manual on Conflict Management for Training GMU Missionaries." D.Min. diss., Trinity Evangelical Divinity School, 1990.

Park, William B. "The Strategy for Local Church Missions." D.Min. diss., Faith Theological Seminary, 1983.

Parshall, Phil. "How Spiritual Are Missionaries?." Evangelical Missions Quarterly 23, no. 1 (1987): 10-16.

Pentecost, Dwight J. The Joy of Living. Grand Rapids: Zondervan Publishing House, 1973.

Peters, George W. A Biblical Theology of Missions. Chicago: Moody Press, 1972.

Phillips, John. Exploring Acts. Neptune, NJ: Loizeaux Brothers, 1986.

Pink, Arthur W. Gleanings in the Godhead. Chicago: Moody Press, 1975.

Pirolo, Neal. Serving As Senders. San Diego: Emmaus Road, International, 1991.

Rhodes, M. Expository Lectures on Philippians. Philadelphia: Lutheran Publication Society, 1882.

Rice, John R. Prayer - Asking and Receiving. Murfreesboro, TN: Sword of the Lord Publishers, 1942.

Rogers, Patrick. "Hopeful in Spite of Chains." Biblical Theology Bulletin 12, no. 3 (1982): 77-81.

Salamone, Frank A., ed. Anthropologists and Missionaries. Studies in third world countries. Williamsburg: College of William and Mary, 1985.

Saucy, Robert L. The Church in God's Program. Chicago: Moody Press, 1972.

Schaeffer, Francis A. The Great Evangelical Disaster. Westchester, IL: Crossway Books, 1984.

Sisk, Don. Joyful Giving. Milford, OH: John the Baptist Printing Ministry, 1992.

Stanbery, Robert B. "The Role of the Senior Pastor In Influencing His Congregation Towards World Evangelization." Th.M. diss., Dallas Theological Seminary, 2000.

Strauss, Lehman. Sense and Nonsense about Prayer. Chicago: Moody Press, 1974.

Thornton, Leo M. "A Study of the Missionary Call as Found in Acts of the Apostles and in Modern Missionary Biography." B.D. diss., Western Evangelical Seminary, 1952.

Vine, W. E. Vine's Expository Dictionary of the New Testament Words. McLean, VA: MacDonald Publishing Company, n.d.

Whyte, Alexander. Lord, Teach Us To Pray. Grand Rapids: Baker Book House, 1976.